EIGHTY MILES
FROM A DOCTOR

EIGHTY MILES
FROM A DOCTOR

In the Depression, a young couple meets the challenges of cattle
ranching and raising a family in remote Dubois, Wyoming.

ESTHER MOCKLER

WIND RIVER PRESS

Editing by Laurie Rosin
Book design and production by Tabby House
Cover design by Pearl & Associates
Manufactured in the United States of America
Library of Congress Catalog Card Number: 97-60611
ISBN: 0-9657411-0-9
Congoleum, Pepto Bismol and Vaseline are registered trademarks.

WIND RIVER PRESS
1155 Bogey Lane
Longboat Key, Florida 34288

DEDICATION

I dedicate this book to
Frank C. Mockler,
my husband, my lover and my friend,
who shared this adventurous journey on the ranch.

CONTENTS

INTRODUCTION

WHAT PROMPTED ME TO WRITE *Eighty Miles From a Doctor* was a question my fourteen-year-old grandson, Frank, asked his mother in 1970: "What makes Mommo tick?"

His mother said, "Why do you ask?"

"Mommo has done so many different things. She spent twenty-nine years on a cattle ranch, had a radio program, learned to make pottery on a wheel at an age when others quit, and is now all excited about living in American Samoa, where Boppo will be lieutenant governor."

To live on a ranch was at the bottom of my priority list. All was changed when I fell in love with the tall, handsome, adventure-seeking Frank Mockler. I would have gone with him to the North Pole to raise tomatoes had he suggested it.

Having been raised on a farm, I was knowledgeable about the mundane skills that would be applicable to a ranch. I liked the space and the environment of a farm but was frustrated with its confinement—no time for play or travel. Perhaps my mother's litany "Esther will do it" and my guardian angel provided me with the courage and wisdom to meet the many challenges in store for me as a rancher's wife.

Our five lively children regularly tested our ingenuity. You may find some of our forms of discipline amusing, others you may not. Our children were not raised by Dr. Spock's permissive method.

Being eighty miles from a doctor was the most disquieting and frightening of all the demands on me. The pluses were Frank's and my ability to expand our horizons. I found mine serving as a trustee on the

xi

local, county, state, and national library boards and through my state church activities. I joined Frank in his involvements in the Wyoming Stock Growers organizations and his serving in the Wyoming state legislature, which eventually led to his post in American Samoa.

After you have read about my twenty-nine years on a ranch, you—and my grandson Frank—may be able to tell what makes Mommo tick!

1

THE BEGINNING

HOW DID A SIXTEEN-YEAR-OLD GIRL, who vowed before her kith and kin never to marry a farmer, eventually end up on a cattle ranch in Wyoming?

I grew up on a farm near Wisner, Nebraska. I enjoyed and related to my surroundings, but hated the confinement. The responsibilities of living on a farm left no time to travel or to explore other lifestyles. The farthest I got away from home was a ninety-mile shopping trip to Omaha.

I was sure I would never marry a farmer when my high-school sweetheart and I planned to wed. He would earn his pharmaceutical degree after my second year at college, and we would be married that summer. My father was so pleased with my success at the University of Nebraska, however, that he told me I should stay in school for two more years and get my diploma. This interrupted our marriage plans, and the romance eventually ended.

Later, I knew I wouldn't marry a farmer when I became engaged to an engineer. I didn't know that my guardian angel had others plans, which would be set in motion in 1928 at the end of my junior year.

In the first part of May, my sorority elected a member to attend the national convention. It was customary for the president to go, but she was unable to attend. I volunteered to be considered, and another member was also nominated. At the meeting, the two of us were asked to leave the room while the vote was taken. Two ballots each ended in a tie. On the third ballot, I lost by one vote.

I didn't mind losing until I learned why I had lost: Four girls had decided I had enough recognition on campus. According to them, the sorority didn't need to add to my kudos by sending me to the convention. I became angry and disillusioned. We had always been encouraged to get involved in campus activities to enhance the image of our sorority. Now I was being punished for doing so. The conniving behind my back sickened me.

I was not prepared for this kind of rejection. When I lived on the farm I had gone to a one-room school and been the only girl in the middle of three classes. My playmates were boys; I never had a girl-friend until I was thirteen years old. Naive, I assumed that girls handled arguments the same way boys did: by confrontation, not plotting in secret or to gain vengeance.

Two weeks later, at the annual university May Day festivities, I was chosen to be a member of Mortar Board, a women's honorary society. In fourteen days, I had been both rejected by my sorority and honored by my peers for my extracurricular activities!

All summer long I mulled over this dilemma. Finally I decided that I had been too serious and dutiful my first three years at the university. I had been reacting to events instead of creating them. There had been no time for carefree and spontaneous adventures. I had only one more year to enlarge my horizons and explore new activities because I planned to get married after graduation in June. By the time I returned to school in the fall, I was determined to play, have fun, and be in charge.

Being well-known on campus, I received many party and dance invitations. Because my fiancé lived in California, I needed an escort. I loved to dance and didn't want to miss that. This year (being in charge) I decided to date new men, and I set my own qualifications for them. The first event for which I needed a date was Homecoming. I asked my sorority sisters to contact their dates and find a fellow for me who was tall, dark, and handsome and could dance. My sister Mabel's date said, "There is a guy at my fraternity who just fits the bill. I will ask him and let you know."

The young man accepted, but a few days before Homecoming he got cold feet. "I've been had," he told his fraternity brother. "Any senior girl who needs to be fixed up for Homecoming has got to be a bore. I am going to break the date."

"You can't do that," my sister's boyfriend protested. "I know her, and she's pretty and fun. If you're so worried, why don't we double date?"

"No!" my blind date said. "If I *have* to go, I'll take my own car. That way, I can come home whenever I please."

On Homecoming night all the girls in our house had been picked up, but my date had not arrived. I waited another half hour, then told the housemother, "I wanted new experiences this year, but being stood up is not one of them. I'm going to bed!"

As I reached the upstairs landing, I heard the doorbell ring. My housemother informed me that my date had arrived. I took my time coming down the wide stairs that faced the front door, for I was piqued at my date's lateness. He watched me, and I watched him. I saw a slim, six-foot two, handsome man with black, curly hair. He saw a pretty young woman with corn-silk colored hair and bright, merry blue eyes.

When I reached the door he said, "I'm Frank Mockler."

"I'm Esther Heyne."

There was an immediate attraction. After the dance, my one-time reluctant suitor took me out for a bite to eat.

In the beginning of the school year, sororities customarily invited a fraternity for a Friday night get-acquainted dance. The Friday after Homecoming, my sorority chose Frank's fraternity. I wondered if Frank would come. I was pleased when he did and felt especially happy when he asked me to be his date at his fraternity's fall party. I thought, *Now I have met a fellow I like. He'll go with me to dances.*

The following Monday Frank called to invite me on a picnic.

"I don't know," I told him. "We have our sorority meeting tonight."

"Can't you miss it?"

I thought a second or two. *Why not?* I decided. I had never missed a meeting before, and I was intrigued by the wacky idea of a picnic in freezing weather. I said I would go.

Frank asked me to get a date for his friend, Bob, and they would pick us up in fifteen minutes.

I got a freshman for Bob's date, and the four of us drove to the Blue River, where a man kept boats for hire. He had already put up his boats for the winter season, but somehow Frank and Bob convinced him to get one out for us. We rowed up to a picnic spot, where we gathered wood and made a big fire—as much to keep us warm as to roast hot dogs and marshmallows. Bob had a good voice, and we joined him in song as we drifted back to the boat dock.

The next Monday, Frank called again and asked me to go to a movie with him. I didn't hesitate this time and said I would go. When I asked the president to be excused, she asked, "Esther, what's happened to you? I don't understand. You know it's your duty to attend the meetings."

She excused me, but that night the sorority created a rule that fined an absent sister fifty cents. The next Monday I went to another movie with Frank and happily paid my fine. He was worth the fifty cents.

Frank and I had no romantic intentions. We both wanted someone to play with and have an attractive date. Besides, Frank had two more years of college, and I was getting married in June.

At Christmastime, when I went home to Wisner, Frank traveled to El Paso, Texas, for a fraternity meeting. He sent me a picture of a bird that had real feathers attached to it. My fiancé sent me a diamond pin. My mother remarked, "You make more over that dumb picture than you do over this beautiful diamond pin."

"I think Esther is falling in love with Frank," my sister Mabel told Mother. "You ought to see them dancing together!"

Naturally, I told Mabel she was all wrong.

After the holidays, I continued expanding my horizons. Frank took me to his swim meets, where he was the champion backstroker. We attended the Nebraska unicameral legislature; my uncle was a member. Frank and I found all the little cafés that had dancing, one being the outdoor pavilion at Antelope Park which charged ten cents a dance. I went to a different church every Sunday and learned that they all believed in God but had different rules to remind them of it.

By April of 1929 I realized that Mabel was right; I *was* in love with Frank. I was in turmoil because my wedding was only two months away. Finally I knew that I had to confide in someone. I went home and told my parents what was happening. They decided that it would be best if I went to California and saw my fiancé in his surroundings. I was overwhelmed by their solution; sending me would be a financial sacrifice for them.

During Easter vacation I went by train to California. When I saw my fiancé standing there waiting for me, I knew our romance was over. He

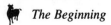

must have, too, for he never once mentioned our wedding plans. I am sure that his cousin, who was also attending the University of Nebraska, told him what seemed obvious to all who saw Frank and me together—that we were in love.

Frank called me when I got home from California, and I told him that I wasn't going to be married. Later he let me know how much that news pleased him. About 10:30 one weeknight, one of the girls who had a room at the front of the house rushed to my room.

"Esther! You're being serenaded! A dozen guys are outside singing love songs and asking for you!"

The whole neighborhood and sorority enjoyed my thrill. What a guy! I knew that living with Frank would be full of surprises and fun.

But what was I going to do while he finished school? No one ever thought of getting married while still a student. I would have a teacher's certificate to teach history and English when I graduated, but that wouldn't do me any good—I didn't have a job. I had not put my name in the university Teacher's Placement Bureau in January. I had missed out on all the placements.

I went to see the bureau, but they had no vacancies. My only hope was that someone would move or change jobs, which sometimes happened in late August. Worse, I had given up my summer job in the drugstore in Wisner the year before. Now I had to find some source of income until a teaching position came through. One of my high-school chums was the dietician in a hospital in Omaha, and she needed an assistant to prepare special diets and help the cook. I took the job. It came with the fancy title of Assistant Dietician but with the pay of a flunky. With board and room included, I had a little left over, which I saved until I could get a better position.

In mid-August my guardian angel took charge once more and found a teaching position for me seventeen miles from Lincoln. Every weekend I stayed at the sorority house to be with Frank. Much of our time was spent meeting his relatives in Lincoln as well as his mother and brother and his brother's wife in Omaha. Some weekends we drove to my home in Wisner to be with my big family.

Frank graduated in June of 1930. He gave me an engagement ring for my birthday. We would get married after he and a fraternity brother returned from their work on a freighter, which would take them around the world. That would take a year, so I had to make other career plans—

I had not renewed my teaching contract. I liked teaching but felt inhibited by the limitations on innovations. When I had been in California the previous year, I learned that some stores had on-the-job training programs in merchandising. I liked selling, and I could live on my salary and be on the West Coast when Frank got back from seeing the world.

My college roommate and I decided to go to our sorority convention in Seattle in July. We joined the special sororities train and arrived in Seattle in midafternoon. As we slowly detrained, I heard someone say, "I wonder who those two good-looking guys are waiting for."

I wasn't interested; I already had my good-looking guy.

Someone else said, "Whoever they are waiting for hasn't come off the train yet."

I thought I would see just how good-looking those guys were. When I did, I let out a yell. "It's Frank!"

Why was he there? He should have been on his way to China. I soon learned that the Depression had forced layoffs every time a ship came into harbor. So Frank waited for my train to arrive in Seattle.

After I had registered for the convention and gotten into my room, Frank took me to dinner. We went for a drive up and down the steep hills of Seattle, down to the port, and finally to Lake Washington, where the bright full moon was mirrored on the lake. We stopped and filled our souls with its beauty. After a while, Frank turned to me and said, "Let's get married."

What a day! The first thrill was seeing Frank in Seattle instead of thinking of him on the high seas. The second was to be married in a couple of weeks. We called our parents to tell them of our decision. Frank's mother wanted to come for the wedding. My parents could not, but they sent me money for my wedding clothes. Frank's uncle and aunt wanted to host the festivities. His aunt told me she was thrilled to have the opportunity to do so, for they had no children. All I needed to do was choose the colors, flowers, and menu for the wedding dinner. When Frank's mother arrived, I stayed with her in the apartment she rented. I was like a queen bee being stroked by her workers. All seemed unreal, like watching a movie, but I was in it. Twelve of us celebrated the event on July 19, 1930.

Frank traded in his blue Chevy convertible for a dark blue sedan. I was disappointed. I loved his Chevy and all the good times we had with it, but his mother didn't think it was dignified enough for a married couple. We began our honeymoon crossing the sound to Vancouver at Victoria, where we fished for salmon and toured the area.

Frank had spent ten summers on a ranch with relatives near the deserted gold-mining town of Atlantic City, Wyoming. As soon as we got back to the States we began looking for ranches to buy. We looked at places for sale in Washington, Oregon, and California. After every tour Frank would say, "But it isn't like it is in Wyoming." I decided that Wyoming must be wonderful, for we had looked at several ranches in attractive settings. I was looking forward to seeing the ranch where he had spent ten wonderful summers.

After six weeks of traveling down the West Coast and into Mexico, we headed for Wyoming, stopping in Yosemite, Las Vegas, and Salt Lake City on the way. On the first day of sightseeing in Salt Lake City, I became nauseated. I went to a doctor who confirmed my suspicions— I was pregnant! The only advice the doctor gave me was to drink as much water and as many liquids as possible and try to keep food down for fifteen minutes so I could get some nourishment.

I had been dreading meeting all of Frank's Wyoming relatives. I believed they were eagerly waiting to pass judgment on my qualifications as a rancher's wife. I would probably be tested just as Frank had been to become a rancher. Now, with the ravages of nausea and my reluctance, all I wanted to do was stop the clock. It wouldn't stop, so we left early one morning on our way to Atlantic City. The day was hot and windy. When I saw a sign for a root-beer stand, I said, "I'm thirsty. Let's stop and get some."

"You know you can't keep it down."

"I know, but it will help for a little while."

We stopped and enjoyed the cool, fizzy drink. As we were going back to the car I said, "Wait a minute!" I dashed behind the root-beer shack and threw up all the root beer. It foamed over my face, giving me a moustache and a beard that matched my hair. I wiped it off and immediately made a smaller version of the first one. It looked so ridiculous that we both laughed. From that time on, whenever I felt nauseated, I would say, "I have to make a beard."

As we left the mountains around Salt Lake, the scenery changed. Endless miles of sagebrush-covered hills were canopied by a cloudless azure sky. I expected the scenery to improve when we turned north at

Rock Springs to go to Atlantic City, but it didn't! Now we traveled over a one-lane, rutted dirt road with grass growing down its center. Looking back I could see plumes of dust, like a rooster's tail, a mile long, marking our progress. There was sagebrush to the right of us, sagebrush to the left of us—no trees, no animals, no mountains, for the next forty miles. Where, I wondered, was that paradise oasis Atlantic City?

As we got nearer, the terrain did change. The Wind River Range appeared to the left and north. Atlantic Peak loomed on the right. Quaking aspen trees in the glorious fall colors of yellow and orange grew on the hillsides. After a long three-hour drive, we came upon the ghost town of Atlantic City and the hotel that Frank's cousin Ellen Carpenter operated.

The hotel was a long log building set in front of shimmering golden aspen trees growing on the banks of a tiny stream. Across the road from the hotel was a small meadow bordering a larger stream named Rock Creek. A wooden stoop at the front door of the hotel opened up into a large room. In the left-hand corner was a post office with a small counter and pigeonholes for the local mail. Along the same wall, in the next corner, was an enclosed telephone booth. In between were rocking chairs, where guests could sit while waiting for their meal. Facing the door was a long table covered with a white cloth, already set up for supper. A huge Army Heater Number One from Fort Stambargh, with logs beside it, kept the room warm and cozy. The stove had a flat top with a steaming kettle of water on it.

Five relatives and two gold miners were waiting to greet us. Ellen met us with open arms. She was a small, wiry, energetic, no-nonsense woman, with graying hair pulled into a tight knot on top of her head. An over-all apron covered her long dress. Next was Jim, with a pipe in the corner of his mouth. He was the only married person in the group. His family lived in Lander during the school year, where his three girls attended classes. He was a gold miner and a fur trapper.

Pete was the quiet one who ran the ranch on Willow Creek, and Bud drove the stage to Lander, carrying mail, passengers, and supplies. Edna, a cousin, helped Ellen in the kitchen. Two miners were introduced as regular roomers and boarders.

Shortly after our arrival, we all trooped into the kitchen to sit and watch Ellen and Edna prepare the meal. One of the miners sat on the wood box next to the wood and coal range. From that vantage, he ogled

Ellen, who studiously ignored him. I found a seat next to the back door, just in case I had to make a quick "beard." When supper was ready, we all went back to the main room and took our places at the long table. I prayed that I would not get nauseated. I took a small bite of fish and drank some tea. In ten minutes, I had to leave the table—a dramatic announcement of my pregnancy.

The next morning we left for the ranch. I was eager to see this wonderful place where Frank had fallen in love with ranching. We followed a track through a small grove of quaking aspens and then through the sagebrush. Our first stop was at Rock Creek to look at the graves of some of the members of a Mormon pushcart trek. In late November 1857, a cold, wet snowstorm forced them to seek shelter in the small cove by Rock River. By morning many of the hungry, exhausted, and frozen travelers had succumbed to the storm and were buried there. Two large wagon-wheel designs were outlined with stones. Each spoke represented a member who had perished. It is a haunting, grim reminder of those tragic expeditions.

After an eleven-mile trip, we stopped the car on the crest of a hill overlooking the ranch. "There it is!" Frank said happily.

I was speechless! I stared. In the valley below, in the middle of a sagebrush flat, I saw a square, four-room log house with a sod roof. A pump and a privy were nearby. In a corral was a low shed with a sod roof. Behind the barn was a small stream lined with low willows. Below the building was a green hay meadow. Not a tree in sight! I didn't know whether to laugh or cry.

"So this is where you fell in love with Wyoming?" I finally managed to say.

"See that creek? That's where we are going to catch fish for our dinner this noon." Frank was so delighted to be there, he never sensed my dismay.

When we got to the house, Pete was in the hay field. Frank picked up fishing gear, and we headed for Willow Creek. He caught a few fish, then he handed me the pole to teach me how to cast. After a number of casts (snagging the line in the willow), I gave up. Frank took the pole and caught enough trout for our dinner.

My introduction to Wyoming life continued when the sage chicken season opened. A sage chicken is a grey speckled grouse that lives near the water in spring and summer, so its young can feed on the young willow and sage leaves and insects. In the winter they live in the sage-brush.

The first morning of the sage chicken season, Bud, Frank, and I drove to the ranch where Pete lived. He was the rancher. He was a lithe, soft-spoken man and had been Frank's mentor and protector from the many pranks, tricks, and teasing he suffered from the rest of the family.

Bud was a swashbuckling Lothario. He had many friends in Lander who enjoyed his company in the bars and dance halls on his regular trips to pick up mail, passengers, and supplies for Atlantic City folks.

When we arrived, I was given a pistol and instructions to shoot only the young ones, and only in the head. We had not walked very far when a covey rose. I took careful aim and killed a young bird, hitting it in the head. Pete and Bud were amazed and called it beginner's luck. We soon scared up another flock. Again, I killed a chicken and hit it in the head. It was then that Frank told them that I had learned how to shoot in college when we had gone target shooting on Sunday afternoons. He explained how we would go to a country road, find a bridge across a small stream, and set up tin cans on the railing for targets.

The next excursion was a deer hunt with Pete and Frank. We went in Pete's pickup, which he drove at top speed through the sagebrush. Both he and Frank laughed at my lurching and hanging on to Frank. Suddenly, Pete stopped the pickup at the brink of a deep ravine. We got out and quietly scouted around a small grove of trees but didn't see any sign of deer. A slight sound from across the ravine alerted the men. Soon a deer was sighted running on a ledge just under the hill. Pete motioned to Frank to take the shot. Frank did, and to our astonishment, two deer fell down! They had been running side-by-side, and one bullet went through both of them.

It was noon by the time the deer had been dressed and lugged up to the pickup. Pete built a small fire to make coffee to go with our sandwiches. I went with him to a small spring to get water for the brew.

As he dipped water from the spring into the pot, I said, "Pete, you can't use that water. It's full of wigglers."

He cupped his hand, scooped off the wigglers, and continued filling the coffeepot. "You won't know the difference after the coffee boils," he told me. "They will all go to the bottom."

Later when he poured me a cup of coffee and I took a sip, he asked, "How does it taste?"

"Well," I said, "it's hot."

Jim was my favorite of the Carpenter clan. Having fathered three girls, he was sympathetic to my constant nausea. After Jim learned of my interest in the history of the area, we followed the Oregon Trail in his pickup. One marker on the trail recorded the Fourth of July event in 1836 when ministers Marcus Whitman and Henry Spalding introduced the first wives to the West and the Indians.

Gold was discovered in 1842 but not prospected until 1855 because few were willing to risk their scalp to the roving Indians. Not until Fort Stambaugh was established in 1860 to protect the miners did gold mining reach its peak. The old army stove at the Carpenter Hotel came from this fort.

Jim took it upon himself to teach me about gold mining. We panned for gold in Rock Creek and found a few flakes. Jim was the caretaker of a mine that tunneled into a hill. His pay for the job was whatever gold he could get from the mine. Whenever he needed to buy a new car, clothes for his family, or supplies, he would go to the mine and dig out enough gold to pay for them. When I asked him why he didn't mine the claim and sell the gold and put it in a bank, he told me, "This *is* my bank." Jim also had a small sluice that he had built indoors. He ran gold ore over a mercury slope, which caught the gold and let the rocks go by. We explored old mills and slag piles, evidence of past gold-mining activities.

We roamed the hillside and found arrowheads, mica, asbestos, crystals, and petrified algae. He showed me his beaver traps and the hides he had cured. Frank decided that I should have a beaver coat, so we selected the hides from Jim's store and sent them to Denver to be made into a coat.

One day Jim took us to Christina Lake in the mountains. A gurgling stream issued from the lake. The water was so clear, I could see trout swimming in its depths. "I will show you another way to fish for trout besides with a worm or fly," Jim offered.

He made a snare with a thin wire on a stick. We lay on our stomachs and lowered the snare into the water. The fish could not see the wire, so when they swam through the loop a quick jerk caught them. I found it much easier to catch fish this way than with a fly. Today, those going to survivor schools would welcome the idea. The environmentalists would say, "Put her in jail."

All these excursions made me realize why Frank loved Wyoming. The fishing, hunting, and great open spaces intrigued him and were

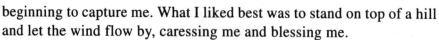

beginning to capture me. What I liked best was to stand on top of a hill and let the wind flow by, caressing me and blessing me.

We went to Lander several times, winding down a dirt road from an elevation of 7,600 feet to 5,000 feet in sixteen miles. On one occasion we looked at a ranch in an isolated valley. While Frank was talking with the owner, I visited with his wife. She told me, "I hope we sell this place soon. I'm going nuts living here. I never see a soul. There is no radio, no telephone, no electricity, no nothing!"

When I got back to the car, I told Frank what the woman had said. I added that I knew I couldn't cope with such isolation either. I hoped he would remember that when deciding on a ranch to buy.

By the first part of November, we still had not heard of any ranch for sale in the area and decided to go back to Nebraska. My continued nausea had taken its toll. I had lost fifteen pounds plus my energy. I needed to find a doctor who would be available when it came time for my delivery. So many new experiences had filled my life in the last four months. I needed to get back to home base to assess them.

2

RETURN TO NEBRASKA

ON OUR RETURN TO NEBRASKA, we spent several days with my parents and three brothers in Wisner. Dad was eager to hear about our ranching expectations. He had always dreamed of owning a ranch, to raise cattle instead of the corn to feed them, but he could never persuade my mother that it was a good idea. She couldn't cope with the isolation and being away from her own family.

My brothers were already making plans to visit us whenever and wherever we got one. Frank's mother, brother, Dick, and sister, Mildred were familiar with the Carpenter ranch at Atlantic City and wondered how I might cope with a similar one. So was I!

For the time being we opted to live in Lincoln, where my sister, Viola, her husband, Norman Hoff, and young son lived. I elected to have my baby delivered by her doctor. We found a new apartment within walking distance of the Hoffs and Frank's relatives.

During the winter the University of Nebraska offered a three-month refresher course for farmers. My father had attended a similar program in 1900. Frank enrolled and acquired useful information on new crops and farming methods.

Soon after our arrival in Lincoln, Frank contacted a real-estate agency. It was February, however, before he received a notice of a ranch for sale. It was located in western Nebraska, in one of the best ranching counties in the West. He liked everything about it until he learned that most ranchers lived in town and drove to their holdings every day. This was not his idea of ranch life. He wanted his ranch to be his home, where his family could be involved with the animals and surrounded by the good earth. He decided to eliminate western Nebraska. We still had no prospects for real estate when Ann was born on April 26.

It is now customary to be hospitalized for no more than three days when having a baby. Back then, we stayed for two weeks of pampering, daily massages, and instructions on bathing, dressing, and handling a baby. The hospital bill was five dollars a day, and my doctor's bill was thirty-five dollars. In two weeks, Ann was on a feeding and sleeping schedule.

I had been home in our apartment for only two days when Frank received a call from Mr. Frankenfeldt, a Lander banker, saying that the Knollenberg ranch on Crow Creek, fifty miles northwest of Lander, was for sale.

Frank went immediately to look at the ranch. It was on a high plateau with lush and extensive mountain meadows. All the fences and corrals were in good condition. A large log house with a fireplace was surrounded by cottonwood and pine trees. Crow Creek supplied the water for the house and cattle and irrigated the fields. The nearest neighbor was four miles away. The nearest town was Dubois, thirty miles up Wind River. Frank had one niggling doubt: Would the ranch be too isolated for his gregarious wife?

The ranch was so perfect otherwise, he decided to buy it and hurried back to Omaha to make arrangements with his banker to pay for the ranch. He was home one day when Mr. Frankenfeldt called to inform him that the Knollenbergs had decided not to sell after all.

Mr. Frankenfeldt sensed Frank's disappointment and frustration and told him, "There is a possibility that you might be able to buy a property in Dubois Country, eighty miles northwest from here. My bank is foreclosing on a loan on a ranch up there. We've been reluctant to do so because the Greens are influential people who've fallen on hard times. If they'd sell the place, they could realize more than the sum of the loan. I'll contact them and suggest it if you are interested."

"I've got to find a ranch somewhere. Yes, I'm interested."

Hoping to visit relatives in Atlantic City, Frank's mother had accompanied him on his return to Lander. Instead, she went with Frank to tour the Dubois ranch. The moment Frank saw the ranch, he knew he had found his dream. The buildings were along the tree-lined Wind

River. Gorgeous mountain views encompassed the spread. The property was three miles from the village of Dubois . . . and that would please his gregarious wife.

His mother made a careful survey of the house, even measuring windows for curtains. When they returned to Lincoln to tell me about our new home, both were vague concerning details. I wondered if it was because of its drawbacks or because they were keeping a wonderful surprise. Whatever the reason, I was eager to settle anywhere and was confident enough in Frank to know it would please me.

The deal was made and signed on June 1, 1931. Possession would be on August 1, 1931.

We gave up our apartment and house-sat for a banker in Omaha for three weeks. During that time we purchased a bed, dresser, and dressing table, a crib for Ann, twin beds for the guest room, and mattresses and springs. We bought a dining room table and six chairs, davenport, lounge chair, console radio, and washing machine.

We spent the remaining few weeks with my parents. Mother suddenly realized that she had never shown me how to make bread. It was fortunate she taught me; fresh bread was not available in Dubois.

Frank and his cousin Lyman Fowler took our new purchases, my cedar chest full of linens, and mother's hand-carded wool quilts in our new truck and car. Three-month old Ann and I would follow later, going by train to Bonneville, Wyoming.

3

MOVING TO WYOMING

OUR RELATIVES WERE CAUGHT UP in our excitement. We would be living 850 miles away, at an elevation of 7,100 feet . . . and eighty miles from a doctor. They also had mixed feelings about our undertaking such an adventure.

My uncle John said, "I told your mother when you went to college that it was a waste of money. All you need to know to be a rancher's wife is how to cook and clean house. Your mother taught you that."

"Uncle John," I said, "when one is married, there is a lot more to do than cooking and cleaning."

His answer was a definite "Hmph!"

Aunt Bertha criticized my mother. "*I* would never allow my daughter to live in that uncivilized state of Wyoming. You know what happened to our sister Martha. She got a ruptured appendix, couldn't get to the doctor in time, and died. She only lived *fifty* miles from a doctor."

A cousin worried that our baby, Ann, would die at such a high altitude. Mother brushed all the dire comments aside, saying, "Esther will do it."

Dad was pleased to have a child fulfill his dream of owning a cattle ranch.

Frank's relatives knew more about Wyoming. Some had visited the ranch where he had spent his summers. His cousin Norma, who had not

Esther Mockler

gone there, was eager to help with our move and decided to spend her vacation at our new ranch. She was to travel with me. The most direct way would have been to go on the Northwestern Railroad to Riverton, but, because she had a pass on the Burlington Railroad, we took a longer route but our extra travels took a half day longer.

We left Lincoln on the first of August. Ann was snug in her basket beside me. As we pulled out of the station, the rails were singing, "Adventure, Adventure, Adventure, Adventure," promising me new experiences and challenges.

We traveled north through Nebraska's rich agricultural lands. At the South Dakota border, we turned west and soon were on the prairie. To pass the time, we played double rummy and read. I had hours to think and assess my abilities to become a cowgirl . . . a rancher's wife.

What knowledge or abilities did I have? I was fortunate to have innovative, progressive parents. When they were married, they had purchased a farm from a homesteader, just like Frank and I were doing twenty-six years later. The first thing my father accomplished was convincing the farmers to get a telephone line built. By the time I was born on June 3, 1906, he was able to call the doctor and a neighbor to help with my arrival.

My maternal grandmother, widowed when her youngest child was only two years old, had to run the farm. She learned about using engines (motors) to help with heavy work. She told her daughters, "I do not want to hear about any of my daughters washing clothes by hand. They have engines to do the work."

My father approved of the idea. He got a motor for mother's washing machine and another to pump water into the house and fill the stock tanks. When he built a new house in 1912 we had running water, two bathrooms, and an electric plant to produce lights.

Although I was a girl, Dad believed I should be aware of all procedures. I learned to milk a cow (but never had to do it), shuck corn, help put up hay by running the stacker team, and understand the nature of hogs, cows, and horses. I observed the butchering of hogs and steers, the curing of ham and bacon, and the making of dried beef.

Mother thought she would be remiss if she didn't impart her skills to her daughters. She made sure we knew how to be sanitary. Cleanliness was next to Godliness. The corners had to be clean; the rest would take care of itself. Dishes had to be scalded with boiling water. A sick person was isolated, and all the sickroom linens were boiled and utensils kept separate.

30

Mother involved us in her cooking and canning. She learned about diets, balanced meals, and new canning methods when she became a member of the Women's Economic Club, sponsored by the Department of Interior after World War I.

For as long as I can remember, I was in charge of my two sisters. Mabel was two years younger and Viola, three years younger. I planned all our playtime and explorations until I was thirteen years old. Dad sold our farm and bought smaller property near Wisner so I and the rest of my siblings could go to high school. I was thrilled about the move one minute and nervous the next. I was a farmer's daughter going to school with town kids who had often called me "hayseed," "country hick," and other taunts when I went to town on Saturdays with my parents. To my surprise and relief, my schoolmates accepted me at once. My self-confidence returned.

Soon my mother found other responsibilities for me. When her cousin Hannah needed someone to help her after her baby was born, my mother said, "Esther will do it."

I helped cook and clean for a week. I was hoping I would be paid five dollars. I got seven dollars—the going wage for an adult. Hannah told me I was better help than any grown-up she had ever hired.

The church needed a teacher for the preschool children. Mother said, "Esther will do it." I had never gone to Sunday School. When the church couldn't find a piano player, my mother said, "Esther will do it."

The summer I was seventeen, the manager of the Farmers Union Store called while I was out on a date. He told my mother that one of his clerks had quit and asked if I would help out. I was awakened very early the next morning and told I had a job because mother had said, "Esther will do it."

As I reminisced about my upbringing, I was grateful for my mother's training and confidence in me, especially the many times when new challenges arose. Then in my mind I could hear my mother say, "Esther will do it."

After our train paused to view the Custer Battlefield in Montana, it turned south into Wyoming. It followed the Big Horn River on its way to Bonneville, where Frank and Lyman would meet us. As we neared Thermopolis, we marveled at the sulfurous emissions of the warm springs. Their residue left a colorful display of red and yellow minerals on the slopes to the Big Horn River. Shortly after leaving Thermopolis, we entered the Big Horn Canyon. The train stopped so the passengers could exit to admire and marvel at the many strata of rocks exposed. Geology students came from eastern universities to study the geological formations. When they were formed, they created a record to show what had happened in each period millions or billions of years before. The deep crevasses were lined with trees down to the clear rushing river's edge.

The scenery changed abruptly as soon as we emerged from the canyon. Once again the high, treeless mesas were covered with the ubiquitous sagebrush. As the train slowed prior to stopping at Bonneville, I peered out the window. I saw a tin-roofed shed shimmering with heat waves. Bonneville was only a shed and a depot where travelers could detrain and go by car to the Wind River country. Bonneville was also the place where the train crossed a deep ravine before turning east.

The night before our arrival, a cloudburst had ripped out the highway bridge across this ravine. Frank and Lyman were forced to park the car in the sagebrush across from the depot and walk the railroad trestle to meet us. The conductor handed down our bags, then he lowered Ann, in her basket, to Frank. Norma and I followed. Frank, evidently overcome by the responsibility of carrying Ann in her basket across the railroad trestle, didn't stop to greet us. We all watched as the six-foot three, slender man, wearing a tall, peaked, light-tan Stetson hat, carefully traversed the trestle with his daughter in a basket on his arm. I held my breath as I watched the two most precious people in my life crossing high above the deep ravine.

We were soon packed in the car and ready to begin the 125-mile journey to Dubois. We drove through the city of Riverton to the top of a mesa and continued northwest to Dubois County. We followed the Wind River, sometimes near its banks, at other times on the top of mesas. We traveled three hours before we arrived at the Red Rocks, where the terrain changed abruptly. The Wind River Mountains were nearer on the left, and the red stratified hills were across the river to the right. The red eroded hills formed many interesting shapes and small canyons. Beyond them were glimpses of the Absorka Mountain Range. Everything was canopied by a cloudless azure sky. We traveled sixteen miles farther before we arrived in Dubois, a village two blocks long. We traveled through it and drove two and a half miles farther west. Frank stopped the car and said, "There it is!"

Across a green meadow was a large log house, the south end covered in hop vines. Four cottonwood trees stood like sentinels in front of it. The house was positioned on the banks of tree-lined Wind River. I was awestruck with the beauty of the setting surrounded by mountains. I held my breath. It surpassed all my dreams.

After a while Frank asked, "Do you like it?"

I looked at him, hugged him tightly, and said, "I love it! It's perfect!"

"There is something I hate to tell you. The Greens haven't moved."

My heart sank. "Oh, no! Why not?"

"They just can't get their stuff together. I told them today if they weren't gone by Saturday, I would have them evicted. I've made arrangements for you, Ann, and Norma to stay at the Welty Inn in Dubois."

"Where are you staying?"

"In the bunkhouse. Mrs. Green feeds us, and we keep busy irrigating the hay fields."

We continued to the ranch and met Mrs. Green. She was small and reminded me of Ellen Carpenter. Grandpa Green was sitting by the side of the wood and coal cookstove, with its side door open so he could spit his accumulated tobacco juice into it. We met the four Green sons, aged sixteen to twenty-four, in the yard. Before we left, Mrs. Green invited us to dinner the next day. I would have preferred that she had spent the time packing.

Our log cabin at the Welty Inn had a double bed, night table, two chairs, and a small stove with a flat top for heating water. A privy was near the river. We could eat in a little café across the highway.

The next day Norma, Ann in her basket, and I took our car and explored Dubois, a town of 250 residents. The quaint, picturesque Episcopal church and a community house greeted travelers coming from the south. On a steep hill behind them was the Dubois cemetery. On the east end of town was the Dubois grade school, made of logs, with outdoor toilet facilities. The two-story, white-clapboard Stringer Hotel housed the U.S. Post Office. Near it was the rambling Legion Hall. There were two garages, two filling stations, two tourist courts, a barber shop, and café. We saw two general stores, Welty's, the Dubois Mercantile, which housed the bank, and two dance halls. A drugstore fronted a very active saloon, which had to be entered from the back alley. We learned that Lander, Riverton, and Casper residents came to Dubois on weekends to enjoy Dubois's disregard for Prohibition and the gambling laws.

The next day we planned to explore some of the side roads leading into the mountains. We were awakened by the patter of rain on the roof. The cabin got cold and damp. We put on all of the warm clothing we had and huddled around the small stove. The heater warmed only one side of the room, where I kept Ann in her basket. When I bathed her, I heated the blankets, towels, and clothes on the stovepipe.

Norma and I had to wile away the time, so we played rummy and read. I had brought along some curtain material for our new living room, and we began to hem it by hand. Soon it was too cold to hold the needle. We didn't want to expose Ann to the rain, so we took turns going out for our meals.

One afternoon Norma came back from the outhouse in a panic. "I lost my diamond ring down the hole!"

"Oh, my gosh! What happened?"

"It was so cold the ring just slid off my finger."

"Can you see it?"

"Yes, but it's down there six feet. I'll never get it back!"

"Yes, you will. You guard the hole. I'll go to the café and phone Mrs. Green and tell her to send Frank and Lyman to the hotel immediately."

I ran to the café. When I contacted Mrs. Green I did not tell her why Frank and Lyman should come. The phone was on an eleven-member party line, and I didn't want to be introduced to the community with our bizarre dilemma.

Frank and Lyman were frightened when they got the message and rushed to the campground in the truck. When I told them of the catastrophe, they convulsed with laughter. We went to the privy, where Norma was dutifully guarding the door, and teased her and laughed some more.

After considering the problem, Frank got the idea of cutting a long willow stick from the growth along Horse Creek. He told me to get one of Ann's big diaper safety pins and our flashlight. After he trimmed the leaves from the willow stick, he put the safety pin through one end, making a hook. While Lyman held the flashlight down the second hole, Frank tried to retrieve the ring with the willow and safety pin. After a lot of advice, chatter, and laughter, Frank succeeded in snagging the ring and bringing it out. Our yells of triumph brought Mr. Welty to the scene. "Is there a problem?" he asked.

When he was told what had happened, he grinned and left without saying another word.

After five days of waiting, we were able to move onto the ranch and examine our possessions. The windows and doors of the long, low log house were painted white. The large kitchen had a pantry. We had a big living room, and the main bedroom had a walk-in closet. Two bedrooms were eight-by-eight feet. The enclosed front porch had a bedroom on one end that was seven-by-fourteen feet. A wooden platform in the back of the house led to a wash house built over the root cellar. Behind the cellar, cherry birch, mountain olive, willows, gooseberry, and rose bushes lined the bank of Wind River. The clear rushing stream murmured in alto tones in its rapid descent toward its eventual destination, the Gulf of Mexico.

Next door was a two-room log house with a sod roof. The sparse growth of weeds on the roof reminded me of an old man's balding head. There were two privies—one behind the house and the other farther downriver. Our noses found the next shed, the smokehouse where hams and bacon were cured. A chicken house was fenced to the river so the twelve birds never had to be watered.

Continuing down the river were a horse barn with hay loft, a cow barn, hog sheds, and another one-room cabin. This cabin was unique, having been built of cottonwood logs instead of pine. It had belonged to the first homesteader of our land. A dilapidated root cellar was behind it. Four lonely cottonwood trees were in front of the building. Was the number four significant? I wondered.

Across from the house was a one-and-a-half story log building that had been converted into a two-car garage. A cupola on the west end of the building housed the bell of the first schoolhouse in the valley. The school had been located across the road and the gulch. At the end of the garage was a long, open machine shed with one end partitioned off for an icehouse, which held blocks of ice in sawdust. A blacksmith, bunkhouse, and granary were nearby.

We discovered a warm-water pond a half mile below the buildings. Watercress growing along its edge was cropped by the mallard ducks nesting there. (Later Frank would dam up the pond and stock it with fish.) Near the pond we found a huge pile of bleached cattle bones. In 1920, the valley had experienced the worst winter storm on record. Normally the valley was free of snow until late January; that year heavy snows came in late fall and covered the usual grazing fields. The previous summer drought limited the hay crop everywhere. Hay could not be purchased at any price, so the cattle starved to death. The pile of bones was a grim reminder of the devastating loss on the Green place. (A year later Frank got a tidy sum from someone who wanted to buy the bones for their calcium.)

Our next excursion took us across the river to the calving shed and hay corral. We thought it would be fun to cross on the swinging bridge. When we saw two boards missing and a guide wire unsupported, we opted for the wagon bridge farther upriver. Steep cliffs behind these buildings were covered with cedar pine and wild gooseberry bushes. The mesa was covered with porous limestone rocks, an indication of thermal activity aeons before.

From the top of the mesa we located two log cabins in a grove a half a mile above the bridge. We had been told that the Green homestead cabins still existed and decided to inspect them. To our amazement, a father, mother, four girls, and a boy came out of the largest cabin to greet us.

Who were they? Why were they living there?

The father informed us they were related to the Greens and had lived there for several years. We had inherited a family! We wondered if we should evict them or let them stay.

Before making a decision about the family, we asked the storekeeper and the banker about them. We were told that the father was an accomplished blacksmith—an almost obsolete trade. He still did a few odd jobs in the area but depended on his huge garden, which produced their summer vegetables and winter supply stored in a cellar. They augmented their diet with wild game and fish from Wind River. Wood was plentiful in the near mountains.

Frank, Lyman, Norma, and I mulled over the situation. If we evicted them, where could the big family go and pay rent? We didn't need the cabins or the land where the garden grew. Frank could hire the man to repair the broken-down machinery left by the Greens. We decided to let them stay until June and gave our extra milk to the children. The Depression intensified, so we let them remain. I hired the oldest girl as a baby-sitter. Later, I hired another daughter and taught her to cook. She was so eager to learn, she became one of the best cooks I had.

Just as the Depression began to ease up, the Second World War began. The family remained for sixteen years.

A few weeks after our arrival, I stood in our yard surveying our surroundings and recalled Mrs. Green's parting words to me: "I hope you will love the Ramshorn Mountains as much as I have."

She didn't elaborate on her feelings, but I know what our ranch setting meant to me then and what it means to me now. Standing in our yard, I had a panoramic view of our surroundings. To the north was the spectacular Ramshorn Peak embraced by two hogbacks where snow frequently gathered to emphasize the summit's uniqueness. Sometimes veils of clouds would shroud the peak. At other times white puffs of clouds would play hide-and-seek around the area.

Fronting the mountains, stratified red hills changed hue all day long from a light red to magenta. To the east, fifty miles away, were the Crow Creek Mountains, which seemed to draw nearer at dusk. They shone pink from the sun's rays, then gradually turned light blue and deepened to dark blue.

Little Warm Spring Creek Mountains peeked behind the bluff across the river. They were more visible when winter came and the crests were covered with snow. The setting sun behind the western mountains controlled the magic changes at dusk. I made a point of watching the brilliant electric yellow and red rays that flashed in the skies. With all this splendor, how could anyone ever be mean or despondent?

4

FIRST YEAR ON THE RANCH

IN RETROSPECT I REALIZE HOW FORTUNATE we were to have purchased a neglected ranch. Cleaning up the place and repairing ditches and fields taught us the importance of constant vigilance and regular maintenance.

During the five days of frustration, as we waited until we could live on our land, Frank hired an elderly couple from Lander who had lost their small property. Mr. and Mrs. Kaiser were of invaluable help, for they understood ranch problems and how to be self-sufficient. They moved into the two-room house. Grant Kaiser earned thirty-five dollars a month, and we paid Mrs. Kaiser thirty-five cents an hour. Frank and I furnished all but their personal needs.

We planned to modernize our house as soon as possible. Before that occurred, the place had to be cleaned. Cousin Norma elected to help Frank and Lyman repair fences while Mrs. Kaiser and I tackled the house. First we washed all the windows and woodwork. We scrubbed floors. The kitchen floor had turned dark brown from many oilings. Crud had accumulated along the walls and corners. A good scrubbing didn't faze the filth. Mrs. Kaiser soaked the areas with lye water, but nothing happened. Frustrated, she asked me to go to the blacksmith shop and look for a spade. I found one, and she soon dug up the crud. A similar situation was found in the pantry, where the cream separator stood. Mrs. Kaiser tackled the wood and coal range using lye and by scraping, she soon had it shining.

The stove was my nemesis; it was like a bronco needing constant vigilance to make it behave. I conquered the top cooking but never the oven, which had no thermostat. The only way to gauge the temperature was to put my hand in it. Too hot, and I would leave the door ajar. Not hot enough? The pies, cakes, cookies, and bread would be colorless. Hot ashes and cinders pockmarked the Congoleum floor.

Frank, Lyman, and Norma cleaned out the sheds, barns, and corrals. The manure was taken to the fields. Fences were rebuilt; posts and gates were replaced. All debris was hauled to a deep gulch that bordered a hay field, to slow the erosion caused by heavy rains and broken ditch banks. We continued this practice and gradually filled in the gulch so that cattle and machinery could cross it.

While we worked that first week, we expected the telephone to ring—calls from neighbors welcoming us to the area. Everyone on our eleven-person party line had a special ring—ours was a long and three shorts. Because ours never rang, I was concerned that it might not be working. I asked Norma to call me when she went to Dubois to buy some souvenirs to take home. Frank and Lyman accompanied her. At every store they stopped at, one of them placed a call. Receivers could be heard going up and listening to our nonsense.

One day, Frank and Lyman locked Norma in the privy and pelted the building with rocks as she begged to get out. Mrs. Kaiser heard them and, disapproving of their shenanigans, felt sure we would go broke in one year. No wonder we were called "the kids who bought the Green place." But we never resented the description. Fortunately, the neighbors soon realized that we were serious about being successful ranchers but would have fun doing it.

We had been in our house two weeks when I heard a loud thumping in the attic. It sounded like kangaroos on snowshoes but turned out to be pack rats! These silver-coated, furry-tailed rodents had a very pungent odor. They were called pack rats or "trade" rats because they were fascinated with shiny objects. A rat might see a piece of tin foil and pick it up. It would see a teaspoon and trade it for the tin foil. They stash cans, nails, scraps of tin, and shards of colored glass in their nests, which are lined with fur from their bodies. We closed off the entrance for the rats, and they never returned.

Modernizing the house became a big project. We made the two tiny bedrooms into one. The pantry became the bathroom. All the brown woodwork was painted white, the walls were papered, and the kitchen was painted a light green. The splintered kitchen and bathroom floors were covered with Congoleum. Bringing water into the house meant constructing water and sewer lines, putting in a septic tank, and adding an electric pump in the cave.

All the craftsmen or supplies had to come from "down below," meaning Lander or Riverton. The craftsmen charged seventy-five dollars for the trip, and we had to feed them and put them up for the night. They brought all the supplies. Because of the great expense, Frank helped the electrician install the motor; he also dug trenches and assisted the plumber. Watching the paperhanger, I learned to make the paste. These experiences gave us enough confidence to perform all future tasks ourselves.

Two cabinets to serve as our pantry were custom built in Lander; the job required six weeks, but the final result was as satisfying as turning on a light in a dim room.

While all the renovations were being made, we hired several extra men to mow, rake, and stack the hay. I had to cook for them. I knew, from observing Ellen Carpenter, that it took much longer to boil potatoes and vegetables in our high altitude. What I didn't know was how much food to cook. For my first noon meal, I fixed what I thought would be enough for dinner and supper. By the time the meal was over, all the plates and bowls were empty. I had to start over for the night meal.

Hay hands liked big desserts. Pie was the favorite. This was fortunate, for the one culinary skill I had was making pies. I made an apple pie one noon. All the men but one—a short, stout, tubby man with reddish hair and moustache, who cooked in hunting camps in the fall—praised it. Hunters claimed he got so greasy that they had to throw sand on him to keep him from sliding out of camp. He was also boastful and vain about his culinary skills. After hearing all the praise for the pie by the other hands, the man daintily lifted the top crust of his pie, picked up the salt cellar, sprinkled salt on the apples, and sniffed, "I always put salt in my apple pies." The men laughed and told me never to put any in my apple pies.

On another day, I decided to make a devil's food cake using my mother's recipe. After it baked awhile, I opened the oven door to check its progress. The cake batter was bubbling out of the pans. I retrieved what was left in the pans and served it as a pudding with whipped cream on top. I didn't know it then, but it was the first of many, many improvisations. The next time I went to Lander, I bought a high-altitude cookbook.

Frank made many trips to Lander, which took three hours to drive the eighty miles. He purchased numerous supplies, including a wash boiler to heat water, a galvanized tub for bathing until we modernized the house, and a secondhand dutch oven still in the family today.

He purchased our first team of horses, named Dorcas and Dolly. An Indian pony named Danny became a member of our family. All our children learned to ride on him. Danny permitted the children to mount by climbing up his legs or his tail. Our young guests rode him. When he got older, he no longer wanted an adult on his back. Whenever he was saddled and mounted by an adult, he would walk to the nearest fence and rub the rider off.

Frank bought two milk cows and had them immediately vaccinated for brucellosis to prevent abortion and to protect humans from getting undulant fever. We used raw milk for as long as we ranched.

As soon as we got the cows, I asked Frank to buy a cream separator and an icebox to store milk and cream.

"We don't need a separator," he told me. "Ellen used flat pans that she put in the cellar, and skimmed the cream off the top."

"Well, *I'm* not skimming cream off milk in the cellar! My mother never did, and neither am I. I guess we will just have to give the milk to the chickens."

When Frank returned from Lander that night, he brought in the smallest separator made. It looked like a toy. It couldn't hold even a pail of milk and had to be bolted to a block of wood. My first impulse was to laugh. I suppressed it, however, for this separator was better than skimming milk.

To accompany the miniature separator, Frank went to a secondhand store, where he found a wooden ice chest. It stood four feet high, held one cake of ice in the top, and had two shelves and a pan at the bottom to catch the melted ice. It, too, was a better solution than my running up and down the cellar steps. One year later, we had a freestanding separator and a full-sized icebox.

After we got the separator, I wanted seamless utensils of glass, tin, or enamel to store milk in the icebox. I accompanied Frank on a shopping trip. I didn't find anything in Lander, so we drove to Riverton. While Frank went his way to make his purchases, I went to every hardware store and looked for my seamless pails. In the last shop, a helpful clerk searched the inventory but couldn't find anything. As I was leaving, I saw some enamel pails on a top shelf and asked to see them. The clerk brought two down. I looked inside and said, "These are perfect—the right size and seamless. I'll take them." The clerk offered to wrap them for me. I said, "Don't bother. They will be easier to carry unwrapped. I'll put my handbag in one."

I walked several blocks down the main street to where our car was parked. Frank was waiting for me. When he saw the pails he said, "What are you planning to do with those?"

"These are our new milk pails. They are perfect—no seams."

"Do you know what they are?"

"No."

He burst out laughing. "Those are sanitary pails! They're used for toilets when there are no bathrooms!"

Maybe so, but they were good milk pails until they got chipped.

By mid-October we were pleased with all we had accomplished. The house was bright and cheery. The grounds were neat and tidy, and Ann was a healthy, thriving baby. But something was missing. No one had called on us. The only woman I had a conversation with was Mrs. Kaiser. The storekeepers and tradespeople were polite and friendly, as they were to tourists. Did everyone think we were too young and frivolous and would soon be gone? Only a few hay hands were there. Not even a member of the family in the Green homestead cabins came to visit.

One Sunday afternoon, I felt so sorry for myself I went to the bedroom to cry, leaving Frank in the living room reading. Suddenly the bedroom door burst open and Frank said, "Get up! Quick! We've got company!"

"Who is it?"

"I've no idea."

I bolted from the bed, powdered my face, put on lipstick, and recombed my long hair. I went into the living room to meet Fred and Gerry Fish, who owned the Circle Ranch six miles below Dubois. Our conversation soon revealed why no one had called on us. We learned the origin of the phrase, "When the work's all done in the fall." The Dubois valley epitomized the phrase because of the short summer season. The ranchers were busy putting up hay; dude ranchers had guests to entertain; tradespeople worked long hours catering to dudes and tourists. Outfitters were taking fishing and hunting parties to the mountains. The timber company was floating railroad ties down Wind River to Riverton. Cattle roundups were beginning. Everyone had guests to entertain. After hearing about all the activity that had to be crowded into a few months, we understood why no one had time to get acquainted.

Fred and Gerry invited us to dinner the following Sunday, and we accepted with alacrity.

The Fishes' other guest was Dick Dennison, an eccentric bachelor who owned a ranch on Bear Creek. During our conversations, we picked up some valuable local philosophy. One, which I immediately assumed as my own, was "Never offend your neighbor, for you never knew when you would need him or he would need you." It didn't eliminate personal feuds, but those were forgotten whenever a catastrophe occurred. Then everyone worked together to help.

This philosophy allowed everyone to choose his own lifestyle, providing it didn't infringe upon his neighbor. Everyone was a friend until proven otherwise. We soon discovered that living in an isolated community was like living in a glass house. Everyone knew what you would do before you did it!

The main source of gossip and information was the Dubois Post Office. Those not receiving rural delivery congregated at the post office at five o'clock, when the stage arrived with the mail, and hung around to visit and exchange news while the mail was sorted.

The telephone party lines quickly related the local gossip. The most reliable source of local news was the telephone exchange. The owner had the unique ability to hear three conversations at the same time. Once, a gentleman was making a long-distance call to Denver. Frustrated with the poor connection he said to the eavesdropper, "Abe, if you would get off the line I might be able to hear better."

Abe answered, "Okay." The connection improved immediately.

Abe was discreet and seldom reported gossip. He was our 911 number and could be counted on to alert us to disasters, arrange emergency trips to doctors, and report national news.

Dick Dennison invited us to his ranch the next Sunday. Frank figured out how long it would take to get there but didn't allow time to get lost. We arrived a half hour late—not a propitious way to start a new relationship. Fortunately, it didn't mar this new friendship. Dick raised racehorses. He had a theory that horses raised in high altitudes would develop a larger lung capacity than low-altitude horses, and thus could win more races. He never conclusively proved his theory.

His barns and corrals were immaculate. One could walk in them barefooted or in evening slippers without getting dirty. His palatial log home had high ceilings. The living room had a walk-in fireplace. The bed headboards and footboards were hand carved and painted in Indian motifs. The beds were so high a footstool was near for a boost. In contrast to the rustic setting was a large room that held a collection of beautiful china, including a dozen rare cups and saucers. Later, when the Depression continued, Dick lost his income and had to sell the cup-and-saucer collection to survive. He never quit growing his famous gladiolus and English bachelor buttons. Our daughter Carolyn still has offshoots of his bachelor buttons in her garden.

Gerry Fish invited me to a luncheon and bridge party. I was excited and eager to meet other women in the community. On the morning of the big event, I checked my silk hose, which I hadn't worn for a while. I couldn't find a single pair without a run! I rushed into Dubois to buy a new pair. I went to Welty's Store, but it didn't handle hose. I hurried to the Dubois Mercantile. Yes, they had some. The clerk showed me a box of black, heavy silk hose. I told him I couldn't use them. He produced another box and said, "Maybe these will do." No, they wouldn't—they were white cotton hose.

I went home and tried to put a pair together. Either the color or the texture was wrong. If I mended a run, it would draw attention to it. I ended up choosing the pair with the least conspicuous run and hoped my new acquaintances would be more interested in my face than my legs.

This introduction to the social life of the valley got me involved in the monthly luncheon and bridge parties. I joined the Episcopal Guild, where I sat on the piano bench with Gladys Purdum. This visit began a lifelong friendship for us. Her husband, Ray, owned the Dubois Light and Power Company, five miles west of our ranch. Gladys often stopped at the ranch on her way to Dubois to visit with me and play with Ann.

In November, I was called upon by the wife of an original homesteader who lived a mile away. She was disenchanted with living so far from Lander and all her old friends. Observing my blond hair and smooth skin she said, "Your lovely complexion will one day look just like mine—all wrinkled. The sun and wind does that to everybody." I didn't realize then how prophetic she was!

In mid-November, late in the afternoon, I saw a cowboy ride into the ranch, heading for the corrals. I wondered who the man was on top of a black Morgan horse, dressed in leather chaps, wearing a Stetson hat secured with a black cord, leather gauntlets, and very high cowboy boots. It was George Cross, who owned a spread on the DuNoir River. He joined us for supper and stayed all night. George had been tempered by Wyoming's weather and isolation to become one of the most astute and knowledgeable ranchers in the area. He began his career when he spent a winter alone on his mother's homestead on the DuNoir when he was only fifteen years old. This man took a paternal interest in Frank. George's counsel, caring, and interest in us would become a silver thread that wove in and out of our lives as long as he lived.

5

FIRST WINTER

OUR FIRST THANKSGIVING MEAL at the ranch would have been forgotten except for my constant learning experiences. We asked the Kaisers to join us. I had made two pumpkin pies for dessert and put one outside with a lid on it to be cool enough to serve with whipped cream on top. When I went to get the pie, I discovered the lid off and a satisfied cat nearby who had eaten all the crust! We ate a warm pie with melting whipped cream.

Our first Christmas season began with an invitation to a party up at Torrey Lake, where there was a small community of five families from New York, California, and Oklahoma. They built their homes on the lower end of the lake, which was fed by springs and had plumbed depths of three hundred feet. Ice could get three feet thick in winter. This provided all of the ice stored in the valley for summer use. The water was so pure, mechanics used it in car batteries. The party was the first gathering Frank and I attended together. We were warmly received. All encouraged us to participate in the New Year's dance in Dubois, the big community affair of the year.

No snow on the ranch for Christmas! What a surprise and disappointment! Snow was plentiful in the mountains, however. Storms would come over the Wind River Mountains in the west and drop all their moisture before they reached our valley. This made it possible to graze our cattle on our fields until March, when snow fell instead of rain.

A white Christmas was so rare it was written up in the paper. A storm would bring snow above us and below us. There was no need for a snow plow for a distance of forty miles. If any snow did come, it quickly blew away.

We drove to the mountains for our Christmas tree and tromped through snow until we found the perfect one. This excursion became an annual event, and we took the children along when they were older.

Most of our gifts had to come by mail. When we first arrived in Dubois, I was warned about Oscar Stringer, the postmaster. He was ornery, unaccommodating, and went "by the book." The window slammed down at precisely six o'clock, customers in line or not.

Oscar was lanky and six feet tall. He had a habit of wrinkling his long nose and sniffling when under duress. His slowness and his Arkansas drawl and idioms annoyed the natives. He wore his clothes until threadbare, which irked the citizens, for his salary was more than any of the complainers earned.

My first encounter with Oscar was at Christmastime. I had ordered a custom-built saddle for Frank's present. The week before Christmas, I asked Oscar every day if the saddle had arrived.

His answer was "Nope."

On the day before Christmas, I arrived at the post office just as Oscar slammed down the window. I peeked through the letter slot and saw the saddle on the floor. I said, "Oscar, I see the saddle on the floor. May I have it, please?"

"The post office is closed."

"But, Oscar, it's Christmas Eve, and the saddle is Frank's present from me. Won't you please let me have it?"

After a long silence, the post office side door opened. Oscar stuck his head out the door and in a low voice said, "I'll give you the saddle if you promise never to tell anyone."

"I promise, Oscar. Thank you! Thank you!"

Oscar took the saddle to the street door, set it down, and opened the door. He looked up and down the street and, when satisfied that no one was in sight, put the saddle into the car.

The day after Christmas, I took him a box of homemade candy and cookies as a thank-you. When I handed it to him he was overcome, speechless. Oscar became a loyal friend all the days of his life.

The New Year's dance was a community gathering. The Swedes who cut the railroad ties in the mountains for the Tie and Timber Company came down the mountain for the dance. Being the new girl on the block, I had partners for every dance. The first was with my new friend the postmaster. He clasped my left hand close to his chest and thrust our right arms straight out. Oscar was so tall, all I could see was the buttons on his wool shirt as we swooped around the dance floor. Fortunately, he was a good dancer, as were his brothers, Albert, Paul, and Carl. I danced with the banker who could do only the toddle. We jiggled up and down, making very little progress. One of the Swedes from Tie Camp approached me asking, "You bane Svede?"

"No. I'm American."

"No matter. Ve dance."

We did, passing everyone as we two-stepped around the dance floor.

Frank came to my rescue several times but preferred playing poker in the back room with a number of our new friends. I was exhausted from all my exuberant dancing by the time we left at three A.M. We stepped outside just as a fight began between two burly young men from two feuding families. These two fought after every big community dance.

Every visitor asks the same question: "Dubois is wonderful in the summer, but what do you do in the winter?"

We enjoyed our winters. Our log house was well chinked and easy to keep warm. A huge woodpile and full coal bin provided fuel for our kitchen range and living-room heatilator. These were banked at night and kept the house comfortable. Ann was snug and warm in her Dr. Dentons, inside a flannel bedroll and covers. We slept between flannel sheets in our flannel pajamas covered with my mother's wool comforters.

We didn't have much livestock yet, so Frank and Grant Kaiser could manage the feeding. They repaired machinery for summer use. I discovered that many women were gourmet cooks. They willingly shared recipes, which I practiced preparing in the winter.

Frank and I were avid readers. We joined the Book of the Month Club and subscribed to numerous magazines and the Dubois, Lander, and Riverton newspapers. The radio provided our entertainment at night. We heard Fibber McGee and Molly, Fred Allen, Burns and Allen, Amos and Andy, Rudy Vallee, Seth Parker, and others.

We spent hours with Ann, who was eager to learn. Frank read to her every night. He would continue storytelling with all the children until they learned to read. I spent days with Ann. She learned to walk at nine months and wore training pants.

To break up winter months, we promised ourselves to take a vacation alone every year. Our first vacation was a weekend to Casper, Wyoming, two hundred miles away. We went to a movie and called on the banker who had transferred funds for our purchase of the ranch.

The first year on the ranch we subscribed to the Omaha *World Herald* for international news. Imagine our surprise when we read that the recipe for the famous U.S. Senate bean soup had been contributed by Senator Dubois from Ohio, the very same man that our town of Dubois had been named for. I saved the following article including the recipe.

> *Not only did Senator Dubois a half a century ago, decree that bean soup should be on the menu, but he even decided what sort of bean soup it would be. Here's the official recipe:*
>
> *Bean soup recipe (for five gallons): Cook the beans dry after cleaning them. Add 2 pounds of ham and the ham bone. When brought to a boil add one quart mashed potatoes. Stir till thoroughly mixed. Add (chopped together) 5 onions, 2 stalks celery, 4 pieces garlic, 1/2 bunch parsley. When these have been brought to a boil, put container over slow fire and allow to simmer one hour before serving.*

Very curious as to why our little town had been named after a senator from Ohio, I contacted original pioneers of the valley for information. I learned that the request for a name for the Wind River Settlement began in 1889. Charles Smith petitioned for a post office to be located where Horse Creek ran into Wind River. He asked a young lawyer from Lander, who had a homestead below the present site of Dubois, to help him. The young lawyer was William L. Simpson, father of a later governor and U.S. senator from Wyoming and grandfather of Alan Simpson, the senator from Wyoming.

The petition asked that the new post office be named Tibo, a Shoshone Indian word meaning "stranger," and a name the natives affectionately called the Ft. Washakie Episcopal missionary, Father Roberts.

The petition was referred to General Dubois from Idaho, who was chairman of the Post Office Committee. He rejected the name of Tibo and named the settlement after himself.

The other question often asked by visitors was, "What is the weather like?" Certainly not what we expected. It was rare when the wind didn't blow from the west. In the summer the days were long and hot until five o'clock. Then they cooled quickly, and by evening a sweater felt right. We always slept under a blanket. We could expect a snowfall that would quickly melt the first week of September. It ended most of our garden products, but many flowers kept blooming.

Falls were glorious with the aspen trees' golden leaves shimmering among the dark green pines on the mountains.

We experienced our coldest weather in February and March. Temperatures could drop to thirty-five or forty degrees below zero. There was no wind. The smoke from chimneys rose straight up. Snow crystals glittered in the air. The gurgling river sounded loud under the plume of fog above it, outlining the river's course for thirty miles. One could hear dogs bark, cows bawl, horses neigh, and people converse from a mile away. Steam rose from the horses and cows and people's noses and mouths. It was an eerie experience.

Cattle had to be fed every day regardless of the weather. Frank and his hired hand took the hay to the feeding grounds in a hay wagon. In subzero weather, the men wore fur caps with earmuffs and a handkerchief across their nose and mouth; deep breaths in subzero weather could freeze the lungs. The cows sensed this, for they approached the scattered hay slowly.

The low temperature never lasted for more than two days. Then the wind began to blow, raising the temperature. The wind was much more threatening and unbearable than the low temperatures.

Our spring moisture came in the form of wet snow in the morning that melted by midafternoon, making a quagmire of our yard. Plowing was done on dry days in May. No planting began until the end of May.

Summer came overnight on the first day of June. Leaves would burst forth. Bluebirds and meadowlarks arrived, and baby ducks appeared on the pond.

6

MY FIRST PACK TRIP

IN MAY WE WERE DINNER GUESTS of fishing and hunting outfitter Louie McMichael and his wife, Gladys. Louie soon learned that Frank enjoyed big-game hunting.

"Have you ever killed a bear?" he asked.

"No," Frank replied, "but I'd like to sometime."

"The bear season opens the first of June. Why don't you go on a hunt with me?"

Frank thought a minute and said, "I think I can. It's a good time for me. My crop will be planted by then."

Louie turned to me. "You come along, too, Esther."

"I don't want to kill a bear," I told him.

"You don't have to. Come along to enjoy the beautiful scenery."

While I was thinking about it, Frank said, "I want you to go. Mrs. Kaiser can look after Ann."

I was excited about getting into the mountains again. Louie's camp was on Frontier Creek. He went ahead of us to bring in horses, put up tents, and make a rope corral for the horses. The next day we followed in our truck, bringing our bedroll, saddles, and extra clothes. We zigzagged through sagebrush until we saw a trail along Frontier Creek that led to Louie's camp. Our tent was set up in the trees along the creek, where the music of the swift, clear stream would lull us to sleep.

Louie cooked a good meal over the open fire. By the time we finished eating, night had fallen. We sat on the bank of the river and watched the moon light up the mountain in the west. The only sound was the murmur of the water flowing over the rocky bed of Frontier Creek. Not a word was spoken, for we were in awe of the beauty and being in touch with something much greater than ourselves.

Very early the next morning, the sun cast a rosy glow over the western mountain. After breakfast we saddled our horses, then went to look for that unsuspecting bear. We rode along the creek for three miles before we crossed it into bear country. Louie cautioned us not to talk, sneeze, cough, or even sigh, for any human noise would spook a bear. I rode in the rear. Once, I cleared my throat, and Louie turned his head, glared at me, and put his finger to his lips.

There was no sign of bear tracks when we stopped for a lunch of Hershey bars, without nuts! A short time later we saw the tracks. The men checked their guns. We were off once more, staring at the ground as we trailed the tracks. All feeling of excitement left me. I was bored. All I wanted to do was get off my horse and put my legs together.

Finally the tracks took an abrupt left onto a steep mesa. Louie declared it was too late in the day for us to follow them. End of the bear hunt. I got off my horse and decided to walk awhile on our way to the campsite. I got off and on several times. I was off when we reached Frontier Creek and had to mount to cross it. I picked up the reins and put my hand on the saddle horn and my foot in the stirrup, then rested while trying to gather enough strength to mount. My horse, as sick of me as I was of him, turned his head and bit my buttocks. I flew up into the saddle, and off we went.

As soon as we got out of Frontier Creek, my horse trotted the next three miles as fast as his long legs permitted. When we got to camp, I dropped off my horse, tied him to a tree, stumbled to our tent, and collapsed on my bedroll.

When Frank and Louie came, they took care of the horses, then came to see me. Frank asked, "Are you okay?"

"No! I want to die. I hurt and ache all over."

Louie said, "You'll perk up after you eat something."

He got a fire started for our supper, and after a while he came to our tent with a hot buttered whiskey in an aluminum cup. He handed it to me. "This will make you feel a lot better," he predicted.

I took a sip of whiskey and burned my mouth on the aluminum cup.

Louie laughed. "That will teach you never to drink anything hot from an aluminum cup in camp."

When he saw the look of rage on my face, he backed away. It was fortunate he did, for I was about to throw the hot whiskey in his face. I recovered, though, and forgave him.

Although we were disappointed not to get a bear, we were philosophical enough to know that not all hunts are successful. An elk hunt several years later with Frank, Louie, and me had a better ending. We worked our way through the trees toward an open area. One minute I was excited, the next minute I was nervous, wondering if I would get "buck fever" (paralyzed) when it was time to pull the trigger on my rifle.

Soon we saw a herd of thirty or more elk grazing in the valley below us. I was given the privilege of having the first shot. I dismounted and removed my gun from the scabbard.

Frank sensed my nervousness. "Take it easy," he told me. "You have lots of time. Now remove your gloves and get a sight on the bull. When you are ready to shoot, aim for his heart so you won't ruin any of the meat."

My heart was pounding loud enough to alert the elk. I calmed myself by taking three deep breaths. I took careful aim and hit the bull. He turned slowly and fell. The shot alerted the rest of the herd, and it stampeded to the trees on the hillside. I watched as Frank and Louie took shots at the elk crossing an open space in the timber. Having had no luck, Louie said to me, "Why don't you try to hit one?"

I reminded him that I already had my elk.

"Try anyway."

I noticed that as the elk crossed the open space, they reminded me of a shooting gallery at a carnival. I timed the crossings, took aim, and much to our amazement, hit one.

"I'll be damned!" Louie exclaimed. "I can't believe it! We've got another Annie Oakley!"

The next surprise came when Frank and Louie dressed out my bull and discovered I had hit it in the heart. I never went on another hunt. How could I have ever topped that performance?

7

THE DUBOIS RODEO

THE DUBOIS ONE-DAY RODEO was scheduled for the last Saturday in July and was celebrated with such gusto that we let our hay crew off for two days—one for play and one to recover.

The rodeo was a local production. Bucking horses, steers, and calves came from the ranches. The pickup men, who rescued the riders, were two ranchers. They were dressed up for their starring roles in high cowboy boots, fancy long leather gloves, blue chambray shirts, red kerchiefs, and Stetson hats. The participants were local cowboys and dudes. Spectators were decked out in Stetson hats, Indian beadwork, and southwest silver and turquoise jewelry. There was a small grandstand, but most people preferred to sit on the hood of their car or stand by the fence, where good-natured raillery was carried on between the performers and spectators. These remarks sometimes produced unexpected results, such as the one in 1932.

During the calf-roping event, one cowboy from the sidelines yelled, "I can rope better from a car than you just did from your horse."

"I'll bet you five bucks you can't," the roper retorted.

"I'll take that bet," said the challenger.

The challenging cowboy contacted his friend Bill Fleischman, from Chicago, who owned a long blue sports car with its top down. They removed the right front door of the car so the roper would have more room to stand on the running board while roping. When the calf left the

57

chute, Bill zoomed the car forward in a cloud of dust. When he caught up with the calf, the cowboy twirled his rope for the catch. He missed when the calf turned abruptly to the right. The car sped on. The crowd whooped and hollered, showing its approval of a good show.

After the rodeo was over and everyone had eaten, the crowds from Casper, Riverton, Lander, and the valley gathered at the three dance halls for live music. The streets were full of revelers going from one dance hall to another. On this night, no one was a stranger. The camaraderie may have been heightened by Dubois's disregard of Prohibition and gambling restrictions.

Revelry continued until early morning. The ranchers were the first to leave; the animals needed to be fed and the cows milked.

The rodeos continued until World War II began in 1942. We didn't know it then, but we had witnessed the end of the Old West in Dubois.

8

THE DEPRESSION

THE DUBOIS VALLEY RESIDENTS probably survived the Depression years with less trauma than congested areas. Never having had access to the amenities of life, we learned to depend on our resources for entertainment and amusements. Fortunately, most people owned their own homes and businesses and were not harassed with loan payments. When the U.S. government declared a moratorium on banking, the Dubois bank had to close. It paid off all the depositors, and the owners netted a profit.

Acquiring cash was difficult. Wages were very low, but so was the price of food, clothing, gasoline, and other commodities. A few tourists, dudes, hunters, and fishermen injected a bit of cash. The Wyoming Tie and Timber Company payroll also put cash into circulation.

The Depression was in some ways a blessing. It gave us time to hone our skills as ranchers, to become self-sufficient and frugal, to work and play together, and to formulate our philosophy of child raising.

The first do-it-yourself venture for Frank and me was paperhanging. The cookstove and the living-room heatilator used some coal for fuel and produced smoke, which stained the walls and made repapering the living room necessary. My earlier observation of the process convinced me that it was easy.

My jobs were to choose and measure the amount of paper needed, cut the lengths, and smear on the paste. I had purchased the special brush for smoothing the paper to the walls. Frank was to apply the paper. During our initial renovations, we papered the ceiling because of its poor condition. In order to reach it, Frank got a long, ten-inch-wide plank and set it on two log stumps. Our hired man walked ahead on the plank, holding the partially folded paper, while Frank smoothed it on the ceiling—at least that was the plan. A third of the way across the plank, however, the board began to sag from the men's weight, and Frank couldn't reach the ceiling. I watched the prepasted strip loosen and drape over the men's heads. My laughter was not appreciated. A third log situated in the middle of the plank solved the sagging problem.

I cut the wall lengths, which Frank could easily apply while standing on the floor. When he reached the end of the living room, he accused me of cutting the strips too short. Remeasuring revealed that the wall was four inches higher at that end of the room! When the papering was done, there was a four-inch piece of wallpaper left.

No food was thrown away. It was the genesis of what Frank called "icebox soup." In the winter we had no access to fresh vegetables and used canned ones instead. I saved the liquid and any leftover vegetables in a pot in the icebox. Once a week, I added noodles or rice or spaghetti, herbs, onions, and leftover meat for soup. If there was no meat, I pureed the leftovers and added cream.

Bacon was a breakfast standby. I saved the grease for frying. When too much began to accumulate, I remembered that my mother used her grease to make soap. I wrote to her, asking for instructions. She informed me that I would need a can of lye and that the directions for making soap was on the label. The result was good, and I used the soap in the laundry.

One year we received a very heavy, flat cardboard box. I thought it would be an ideal base when cutting the soap into bars. I placed the box on the table, then my cook helped me pour the hot, melting soap into the box. Fifteen minutes later, I noticed soap seeping out of the cardboard and onto the floor. I yelled for my cook to help me carry the collapsing box outdoors. I was unaware that when soap cools, the finished soap floats on top of the lye residue. The lye was dissolving the paper box. The effort involved in making soap was too harrowing, so I never made any more.

Our leisure time was spent exploring the beautiful, fascinating country around us. The first excursion took us to the Dinwoody River area.

We put Ann in her car seat and strapped it to Frank's back. The hieroglyphics on the canyon walls intrigued me and piqued my interest in ancient Indian history, which I would later study. Other times, Frank and his brother Dick went fishing in the numerous mountain lakes and often returned home with a string of six-pound rainbows.

The terrain on the mesa south of our river indicated thermal activity aeons before. Slabs of pure lime were scattered over the area. The *clop, clop* of the horses' hooves denoted hollow cavities underneath. An extinct geyser twenty feet below the surface created a warm pool—a fun place to skinny dip in both summer and winter.

The second summer we took our first trip to Yellowstone Park, eighty miles west of us. The unpaved road wound through the forest to the top of Two Gwo Tee Pass where there was a turnoff to view the Teton Mountains. The sun shone on the rugged peaks, with valleys of snow between them. All were mirrored in Jackson Lake at the base. This startling, dramatic view brought tears to my eyes. In the park, the geysers—especially Old Faithful—and bubbling mud pots from the earth revealed our planet's secrets, never ceasing to amaze me, on that excursion or the numerous trips that followed.

Raising cattle provided our income. Our first herd consisted of sixty-seven pregnant Hereford cows and sixty-nine calves. It was necessary to create a brand that was simple, not easy to alter, and not owned by anyone else. We drew brands for two days, trying to find one not recorded in the Wyoming brand book. We chose the letter "M" with two quarter-circle arcs under it to be used on both cattle and horses.

Several years later, we were fortunate to buy the LU brand, which had originally been owned by Wyoming's first governor, John J. Campbell. We used it exclusively on our cattle but continued to use the M with the double quarter circles on the horses.

Our small valley west of Dubois was originally called the "salt sage flat," used by wild animals for the salty sage that grew there. When the area was developed, the game quickly discovered the blocks of salt that the homesteaders put out for their livestock. The ranchers in the valley formed the Red Flat Valley Association and hired a cowboy to herd the cattle on the combined forest permit. He stayed in a two-room log cabin.

At roundup time, the cattle owners stayed in the cabin for several weeks to sort out the calves, dry cows (those that had not calved), and an occasional bull that were to be shipped to the Omaha market. These cattle were driven the fifteen miles to the owners. On a specified day, the cattle drive began the eighty-mile trek to the loading station at Hudson, Wyoming, half the distance between Lander and Riverton. The ranchers enjoyed the drive. They covered eight miles a day, allowing the cattle to graze along the way. The weather was usually clear, cool, and exhilarating.

One of the ranchers was in charge of the chuck wagon, which was our truck. It was loaded with food, water, utensils, oats for the horses, and bedrolls. The rancher prepared the meals and located the next night's stopping place. The men's favorite campsite was at the warm springs on the Shoshone reservation, where the travelers revelled in the much needed swim. Frank got kidded for taking a fifteen-minute nap every noon after lunch. He would roll up his jacket for a pillow, cover his face with his hat, and drift off to sleep.

Frank, wanting to be sure the cattle were fed and watered at Pine Bluffs, Nebraska, always went on the cattle train to Omaha. Other ranchers from the area had cattle on the train, too, and the men rode in the caboose. The accommodations were primitive, but the camaraderie was great.

I usually drove our car to Omaha. Frank and I would visit with relatives and shop before returning home. These trips often had to be our promised vacation of the year. The cattle drives continued until after the war, when trucking began.

The cattle market during the Depression was a disaster. Our first shipment to Omaha in 1933 netted us five cents a pound! When prices didn't improve, the U.S. government got the impractical idea of paying ranchers a bonus for every cow destroyed, thinking a shortage of calves would force the prices up. Few ranchers participated. *We* didn't. The few animals destroyed were supposed to be buried or burned, but we heard that many carcasses somehow found their way to the Indian reservation, where the people were starving.

We were keenly aware of the pain of the Depression when all the young men began hitchhiking by our gate on their way to the West Coast, looking for work. They would stay at the ranch, wanting a handout and a place to put their bedroll to sleep. Some were college friends of Frank's. We never turned anyone away. Someone told us our place had been marked as an easy place to stay all night and get two free meals. We were glad to share; but when the itinerants became too numerous, Frank made it a rule that to be accommodated, they had to chop wood, a chore none of our help liked to do. Several itinerant reactions to this made a lasting impression.

One summer afternoon, I left Ann with my help—a neighbor and practical nurse who had trained in England—while I played bridge. A young man came to the door for a handout. Mrs. Anderson, a large, tall woman, told him, "The boss says you have to chop wood first."

The hobo said, "To hell with the boss!"

Mrs. Anderson opened the screen door, advanced toward the young man, and said, "To hell with you. Now git!"

The fellow fled and kept looking back to see if she was following.

At five o'clock one afternoon, a man about thirty years old asked for a meal and a place to stay all night. His head was shaved, and he had no tan. He readily agreed to chop wood. He split a big pile into kindling as fast as I could chop cabbage. He split another big pile the next morning. After the man left, our hay hands told us their experience the previous night with the stranger in the bunkhouse. They reasoned that a man with a shaven head and no tan had to be an ex-convict. He was probably in prison for having chopped someone up. The men took turns keeping watch. At midnight the fellow was sleeping so soundly they decided he was harmless and gave up the vigil.

Shortly after dinner one day, a tall, slender man came to the back door and asked for a sandwich to take with him over the mountain. I told him the rule, and he chopped wood for twenty minutes. He returned to the house for his sandwich. He peered in the sack I handed him and saw two sandwiches, some cookies, and an apple. He looked at me and said, "My goodness! I didn't expect so much. I'll go chop some more wood."

Toward the end of the Depression, a thin, dirty, and bedraggled twelve-year-old girl knocked on our door. I saw no one else, so I asked, "Where did you come from?"

"My pa and my brother are on the road in a wagon. We was wonderin' iffen you could give up somethin' for our supper tonight."

I filled a paper sack with potatoes, a can of corn, and a can of peaches. When the girl looked in the sack, she grumbled, "Potatoes. Potatoes is all we *ever* git!"

The last hobos came the first year of the war. At roundup time, when Frank was in the mountains, a couple appeared. The man was tall, thin, and dirty. The woman was overweight, grimy, and exhausted. They had no bedroll and asked if they could sleep in our barn. In no way did I want them in the barn. If they smoked, they could start a fire—a nightmare for a rancher. There was no defense against one—it could rapidly spread and destroy all the buildings. I let the couple stay in the small house, where they could clean up as well as sleep.

They asked if they could have something to eat. I fixed some food and sat at the end of the table while they ate. Our labrador, Sheba, lay beside me. Every time the couple made a move, Sheba's hair stood on end, and she bared her teeth. I wasn't nervous only because of the couple's appearance but because of Sheba's reaction to them. I asked them where they were going. When the woman began to answer, the man gave her a vicious kick on the shins. Sheba tensed and rose from her prone position. That frightened me more. On the way out the door, I told the couple that if they wanted breakfast, they had to be at the house by seven o'clock. Frank and I never locked our doors, but that night we did. Sheba stayed inside and I slept with my revolver.

The transients were at the house on time for breakfast. After they finished, I hustled them out to the highway to catch a ride and watched until someone picked them up. If they had any evil intentions—as Sheba and I sensed—they may have been suppressed because of my good Samaritan treatment.

The Little Theater plays and skit nights were very popular. Local talent produced them. The actors were not inhibited by fear of ridicule, criticism, or comparison to professional players and casts.

The first few years, the plays were well-directed by a schoolteacher. After he left, I was asked to replace him. I had directed the senior play in Hickman the year I taught there. I particularly enjoyed training the young actors to become another character. Because I was replacing a favorite and much-loved director, I was jittery and wondered whether I could inspire adults as I had the teenagers.

Frank didn't help, either. He didn't think a play with amateurs would be any good, and he didn't approve of my being gone so many nights for practice. He underscored his disapproval by refusing to attend the performance.

The play was performed well, and it earned enthusiastic applause. So many theatergoers verbally abused Frank for not attending, that he never missed another play.

Spending so much time and energy on a play made the actors want to perform it elsewhere. Lander had a Little Theater, and the actors there felt the same frustration as Dubois's. Soon we were presenting our plays in each other's town. One year I directed the play, *January Thaw*. After the showing in Lander, we were invited to do it in Douglas, 250 miles away. A reporter from the Cheyenne newspapers came. She pronounced it a better production than the one Little Theater in Cheyenne had put on.

Skit nights were reserved for original scripts, which consisted of four or five acts that were either hilarious, well done, or so ineptly performed that they were funny.

Dances were also very popular. They were held every Saturday night in the summer and on special occasions the rest of the year. The music was always live. The American Legion held an annual rummage sale and a masquerade in October. Some of the costumes were picked up at the sale. When our son James was ten, he and his pal, Lyle, went to the sale and came up with an idea when they saw a baby buggy. I helped them with their disguises: James was the "mother" and wore one of Ann's dresses, her high-heeled shoes, and a scarf. Lyle, the baby, wore a lacy cap and covered up with a baby blanket. He had a baby bottle of milk and cried often. Spectators hadn't an inkling as to who they were. They were chosen as finalists to parade around the hall for the judges to choose the winner. James and Lyle won and were given a tremendous ovation. There was one problem: The prize was a bottle of whiskey! This dilemma was solved by the Legionnaires giving the boys five dollars, instead.

Frank and I often attended the masquerades. My favorite guise was that of a clown. I never said a word. Heavy makeup covered my face. No one knew whether I was a man or a woman. Another favorite costume was a Bowery girl. My face was so made up that no one recognized me. Frank's favorite guise was a pirate. His costume was a red handkerchief around his head, a black moustache, curtain ring in one ear, a bright red or yellow rayon blouse, and his old, too-tight tuxedo trousers.

One trait that we acquired—typical of many who weathered the Depression—was to save our money for new purchases or pleasures. If we wanted a new car, a piece of machinery, a horse, a rug, or a new house, we put the money in the bank where it could draw interest, rather than borrow money and pay interest. After enough money had been accumulated, we sometimes found we didn't want the item or need it. When this occurred, we might use the money for an extra trip or an unexpected investment. *If something isn't worth waiting for,* we thought, *why buy it now?* This concept must boggle the minds of the present generation.

9

THE RANCH HELP

THE HELP ON OUR RANCH played a significant role in our lives. The heterogenous mix of itinerant and year-round hands left no room for boredom or complacency. We felt responsible for their welfare for as long as they were with us, but to keep our lives independent, certain formalities had to be established. The men addressed Frank by his first name, but everyone else called him "Mr. Mockler." I was "Mrs. Mockler" to everyone. Titles implied authority and respect—not easy for two very young ranchers to establish. Frank and I were good bosses; we never asked anyone to do something we wouldn't do. We could and would assist or take over when the need arose.

When the Kaiser family left after one year with us, Frank hired a couple who had a two-year-old daughter. Ann was delighted to have a playmate and happily shared her toys and sandbox. On the family's second day on the ranch, I heard Ann scream. I rushed outside to discover that the new girl had bitten Ann hard enough on her forearm to draw blood. I took the tiny offender home to her mother and explained what had happened. "Oh," the mother said offhandedly, "she has a bad habit of biting. She even bites me. I'll tell her to quit."

But the biting continued. Ann became more adept at defending herself. Three weeks later, however, the girl bit Ann on her cheek, breaking the skin. This was more than Frank and I were willing to tolerate. We had to let the man and his family go.

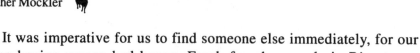

It was imperative for us to find someone else immediately, for our busy haying season had begun. Frank found a couple in Riverton—Casey and Bill Jones. Bill appeared to be calm, sturdy, and in good health. Casey was excitable and volatile, presaging a lot of commotion and amusement.

When hiring couples, the wife's role had to be evaluated also. That responsibility was assigned to me. My university psychology classes proved helpful. I relied most upon the phrases "Do unto others as you would have them do unto you" and "Be a little kinder than necessary." We learned immediately that Casey had been a mail-order bride. She was in her thirties and had come from Kansas City, which is how she acquired her nickname (K. C.). Bored with her life there, she perused mail-order bride-and-groom magazines. One ad caught her fancy: "Sheep rancher, in good health, lonesome."

After an exchange of letters and photographs, Casey was eager to marry the handsome sheep rancher from Wyoming. She wrote to Bill and told him the day and time of her arrival in Riverton.

The three-day train ride gave Casey hours to fantasize about her new life on a sheep ranch, where, married to a handsome man, she would live in her own big house. She dreamed about learning to ride and owning her own horse, and she planned to return to Kansas City some winter, wearing a long fur coat.

Casey got off the train in Riverton. She protected her complexion with a pretty parasol and carried a bird cage. She did not know it, but she came in the midst of the county-fair celebration. She was greeted by yelling Indians in native dress and cowboys riding horses through the crowds of men, women, and children. Worse yet, Bill did not meet her!

Terrified, Casey rushed into the depot, found the stationmaster, and asked when the next train left for Kansas City. It wasn't until the following morning. Casey bought a ticket. The stationmaster took her, the bird cage, and her suitcases to the hotel. As soon as Casey got to her room, she locked the door, shoved the dresser in front of it, and stayed barricaded inside until her departure the next morning. For dinner she ate a few cookies left over from her trip.

Bill had not gone to town recently to pick his mail and supplies, so he was unaware of Casey's arrival. When he finally read her letter, he was devastated. He called her long distance and begged her to return. Casey said she would if he would be sure to meet her.

They were married by the justice of the peace and left immediately for their home in the mountains. After hours of bumping and lurching through dusty sagebrush, Bill told her, "It's just around the next bend."

Casey's heart leaped in anticipation. When she saw her new home, however, she thought she was going to faint. There was no house, no yard, no corral—only a sheep wagon with a horse and a dog tied to the wheels. Bill was a sheep herder!

Casey felt betrayed and insisted on leaving immediately. Bill persuaded her to stay two weeks, at which time he would be going to town for more supplies.

At the end of the fortnight, Bill had been so kind and considerate that Casey told him she would stay in Wyoming if he got another job. That job was offered when Frank was looking for help.

Not long after the Joneses arrived, Bill came to the door early one morning and said, "Casey's as stiff as a board and can't talk! Will you come and help her?"

I said, "Of course," and we hurried to his house. As soon as he took me to the bedroom, he left me alone with his wife. Lying on her back on her bed, she was staring at the ceiling. She was rigid and cold, with her arms tensed on each side.

"Casey, can you hear me?" I asked.

She formed the word "yes" but made no sound and did not move. I thought, *What do I do now?* I asked her if I should give her a massage. She again formed the word "yes" but made no sound.

I ran to my house for some of Ann's baby oil. When I returned, I told Casey I would have to remove her gown to give her a massage. It was a struggle to remove it from her inflexible body. I discovered she was wearing a long, tightly laced corset. I massaged her from head to toe, which relaxed her enough so that she could utter a request for me to read a Unity prayer that was on the chair at her bedside.

After I read it slowly several times, she began to unwind. More massaging and reading finally relaxed her. I put on her gown and read the prayer once more. She fell asleep and slept all day. In the evening, I gave her another massage and read the prayer. The next morning she was her usual excitable, nervous self. She never had a similar episode for as long as they lived with us.

We added two rooms to the Joneses' house. The dividing wall was of pine paneling. The back room had an outside entrance, to be used for my first full-time help.

One would assume that in the Depression there would have been plenty of domestic workers available. Not true in Dubois. When I couldn't find anyone locally, I contacted an employment agency in Denver, which sent me Mrs. Brown. She was a five-by-five Mexican who smoked cigarettes all day long. Her cooking skills were minimal. She knew nothing about roasting meat, and she didn't bake bread. We ate hot biscuits and corn bread. During her free time, she sat perched on a high stool with her full skirt covering her feet. She looked like a huge pear smoking a cigarette.

Casey Jones did not like Mrs. Brown because she smoked cigarettes. Casey insisted she could smell the smoke through the walls in her new bedroom. Casey demanded that Mrs. Brown quit smoking when in her own bedroom. Mrs. Brown refused, saying she could do whatever she pleased in her room. After several weeks of arguing, Mrs. Brown's patience ended. She discovered a knot in the pine paneling, worked it loose, and blew smoke from her bedroom into the Joneses' living area. Bill Jones was more important to the ranch, so Mrs. Brown had to go.

At three o'clock one morning, I heard shots being fired in the Jones house. I sat up in bed and said to Frank, "The Joneses are shooting each other! Go over and stop them."

"And get shot?" he asked me, then went back to sleep.

The next morning, we learned about the explosions; Casey had made some beer that was not fermenting properly. She set the bottles behind the cookstove, where the warmth would start the fermentation process. It did, and popped every single cap, spraying beer all over the kitchen.

The Joneses left a year later after haying season. We managed the next winter with Sharkey, one of the young men from our hay crew. He became enamored of a young woman in town, but her father did not like the young cowboy. Frank was away when Sharkey went to call on his new love one Sunday afternoon. I was concerned when he didn't come home for supper to milk the cows.

By eight o'clock, I called my neighbor to do the chore. I could have done it, but I didn't dare—if it became known that I could milk a cow, the milkers would find countless excuses in the future so they could be late at milking time. (In fact, even Frank didn't know I could milk until after we had left the ranch.)

Young Sharkey finally came to the door at nine o'clock. He was dirty, with bits of weeds on his clothing. The girl's father had gotten him drunk, then put him out of the house. It took Sharkey hours to crawl and stumble home. He was afraid he would be fired.

Frank, guessing that the father's intent was to get the cowboy fired, let Sharkey stay.

In the summer of 1943, we hired our last couple until the war was over. The man was a good worker but an alcoholic. His recreation was to go to Dubois every night and come home in time to go to bed. His wife, Grace, was older and as tough as nails. She had been in rodeo shows, and when that was passé, she learned to be a short-order cook. I asked her if she would work for me. She said she would cook, but do nothing else.

Grace refused to roast, stew, or boil any meat. Everything was fried. I planned menus with her, but whatever we had worked out was never what she cooked and served. She never explained the changes or talked about them. She did it her way, or she threatened to quit.

Grace was extremely possessive of her handsome husband and accused him of having a girlfriend in Dubois. Every night we could hear the doors slamming in their house and the couple yelling at each other.

One evening we didn't go for our mail in Dubois until after supper. In the stack was a letter for Grace. I asked Carolyn to take it to her. When Carolyn knocked on her door, it flew open and Grace shoved a gun in Carolyn's face. Carolyn dropped the letter and ran home. She was trembling and white when she came inside.

In a few minutes, Grace came to apologize for scaring Carolyn. She had thought the knock had been her husband. I dismissed Grace, and she got another job. Her handsome, alcoholic husband left her.

As soon as the war was over, Frank was delighted to hire a highly recommended young man who had recently been married. He was sturdy and knowledgeable about farming and cattle raising. There was no inkling of a soap opera going to be played in the future, but one began a month after the newlyweds' arrival.

Prior to making a trip to Lander or Riverton, I inventoried our household supplies, which were purchased in bulk. I discovered that my fancy canned goods were gone, but I hadn't had guests or a party. An unusual amount of toilet paper, napkins, and laundry and hand soap had also disappeared. Then, recalling that my hens had been laying in an unusually erratic pattern, I knew we had a thief! I was certain that the culprit was the bride, but how could we prove it?

She had easy access to our home. My young cook welcomed the bride's company and especially her willingness to help. On Mondays (wash day) the bride helped the cook fold clothes that needed no ironing. Then she took the clothes upstairs, where the children and I would put them away. Soon the bride was bold enough to steal two sheets off the clothesline.

One day Frank asked me if I had taken some money from his billfold in the top drawer of our dresser. I hadn't. It was time to devise a scheme to catch the thief in the act.

My brother, Cliff, was staying with us that summer. He, Frank, and I gleefully plotted a way to catch her. The drama would have to be played on a Monday, when we knew she would be in our rooms upstairs. In preparation, Frank went to the bank and had the teller, in the presence of two witnesses, mark three five-dollar bills with a punch mark in the lower right-hand corner on the front.

On Monday afternoon, Frank put the marked bills in his billfold in the dresser drawer. Cliff went into our bathroom, where he left the door ajar to permit him to see the dresser. Frank went outdoors, and I was downstairs in the living room with the children.

Soon the bride came into the bedroom, dropped the clothes on the bed, dashed to the dresser, stole the bills out of the billfold, and put them in her pocket. As she turned around, she caught a glimpse of Cliff in the bathroom.

"What are you doing here?" she screamed.

"Watching you," Cliff replied.

The young woman called him every vile name she could think of before she fled downstairs and home.

Frank waited until after supper, when her husband was home, to confront the situation. "I have reason to believe your wife took some money from my billfold before supper," he told his employee.

"I never did no such thing!" she said. "He's lying!"

Frank asked her, "Would you be willing to let me see your purse?"

Her husband interrupted. "I think I should tell you that when we went to Dubois tonight before supper, my wife found some bills on the ground when she stepped out of the car."

"May I see the bills?" Frank asked.

The young man went to the bedroom and got the purse.

Frank said, "Before you show me the bills, I'll tell you what you will find." He described the banker's punch marks.

When the young man saw the marks, he cringed and stared at his wife in disbelief. The bride snatched the bills from her husband, threw them at Frank, and screamed, "Get out! Get out!"

Frank picked up the bills and told the disillusioned young man, "I'm not firing you, but I want your wife off the place tomorrow morning."

When the children heard the story the next day, Carolyn said, "I wonder if she stole money from my piggy bank."

She raced upstairs and came down immediately. "My money is gone! My money is gone!"

The young couple left. When their house was cleaned after their departure, the workers found bags of chicken feathers hidden on top of the kitchen cupboard. The bride not only stole eggs, but she ate the chickens that laid them.

Our full-time help problem was solved soon after this episode. Frank received a letter from a previous worker named Lester, saying he was recently married and would like to come back and work for us. Frank was delighted to have the good-natured, strong, diligent man return. Lester and Margaret came and would remain until we sold the ranch. We immediately modernized their house. Later, we built a new home for them.

Until our sons were sixteen, we always had cousins, brothers, nephews, or friends' sons spend the summer with us. They, along with a motley group of habitual hobos, alcoholics, thieves, and runaways, always helped with the haying. These men brought their own bedrolls with their scant belongings wrapped inside. These drifters were satisfied with a roof overhead, three big meals a day, and a paycheck when they left. The only repeat visitor was an alcoholic who said he liked the boss and the good food, and needed money to get him to L.A.

One worker was a young blond fellow who came without a hat. We always kept a supply of hats for the unwary; the penetratingly bright sun was lethal. We offered him a hat, but he refused to wear it.

The end of his first day of haying, he didn't come in for supper. At eight o'clock, one of the hay hands asked me to do something for the newcomer—he was shivering and his face was as red as a beet. He was suffering from sunstroke. I knew what had to be done, for Frank had endured a similar experience after a long day on a Florida beach. I took him a hot-water bottle, extra covers, aspirin, and lots of water to drink.

The next day, I fed him fruit juice and broth. After he recovered, he decided to leave—wearing a hat.

One year a young, handsome, tall Mexican from Texas arrived for the haying season. He was a good worker, affable, and especially well liked by all the young girls who flirted with him at the Saturday night dance. Everyone agreed he would be missed when haying was over. Something else was also missed—Frank's saddle! When Frank discovered the theft, he immediately notified the sheriffs of Fremont and Teton counties and gave them a description of both the saddle and the thief.

Two days later, the Jackson sheriff caught the Texan when he tried to pawn the goods. Luckily, the sheriff returned the saddle to Frank.

Several summers later, we were duped by another diligent hay hand. When the season was over, Frank paid him after breakfast. The fellow left in his dilapidated car. Midmorning, he returned and knocked on our back door. He apologized for bothering me but said he had forgotten to take his bedroll from our storeroom. Could he get it now? he asked. I told him that he could.

At noon I described the incident to Frank, who cursed. "I saw him put his bedroll in his car this morning. I bet he took mine!" He stomped off to the storeroom. Sure enough, his bedroll was gone.

Several days later our neighbor Paul was telling about a pack trip he was taking with his brother and how lucky his brother was to have picked up a good secondhand bedroll at a bargain price at the Lander Pawn Shop.

"Paul," Frank asked, "by any chance did the bedroll have an eight-by-two-inch blue patch on one corner?"

Paul's eyes widened. "Why, yes. But how did you know that?"

"My bedroll was stolen a few days ago. I had ripped it once, and Esther mended it with some blue canvas. I'll bet it's mine."

It was. Frank got it back. Lucky again.

In 1949, roundup came before the late grain harvest was completed. Lester, our foreman, stayed behind to help finish it before he went to cow camp. He hired a twenty-one-year-old and a fifteen-year-old to help him. I had no cook, so my son, James, helped me with supper. One evening he told me, "Call me when you're ready for me to wipe the dishes," and went in to the living room and sat on the davenport to do his homework.

Five minutes later, white and wobbly with fear, he came to the kitchen door.

"James, what's wrong?" I asked.

"Someone tried to kill me! A bullet came through the window, and the glass shattered all over me."

I was terrified. Who hated us enough to want to kill us? What had we done? Why? *Why?* I turned off all the lights, and this enabled me to see the hole in the window and the glass shards on the davenport. For some reason, I wanted to find the bullet. James and I got down on the floor and patted the carpet. I found the shell under the window drapery across the room. It was a huge bullet—from a German Luger pistol. Just as I found it, someone opened the back door and walked into the kitchen. I froze. Someone was coming to shoot us! Then I heard the living-room door open. I thought, *This is it!*

"Mrs. Mockler," I heard Margaret call. "Mrs. Mockler, are you there?"

I ran to her. "Shhhh!" I warned. "Don't turn on the light. Someone just tried to kill James!"

Margaret sagged. I thought she was fainting. She recovered and whispered, "Someone just tried to kill *me!* I stooped over to feed the cats, and a bullet went right over my head."

In an instant, my terror turned to rage. "Margaret, those darn kids in the bunkhouse are playing with guns! Lester will have to go and stop them."

But Lester was as scared of the wild bullets as we were. "It reminds me of dodging bullets in the war," he said. Nonetheless, albeit reluctantly, he went to the bunkhouse. He found a neighbor's son, who had come for a visit, showing off his brother's German Luger pistol. He and our two young workers were shooting at the logs in the bunkhouse. Some missed and went through the chinking between the logs, into our living room and over Margaret's head.

When Frank came down from the roundup to get Lester, I expressed my doubts about keeping the two irresponsible fellows. He pointed out that it was impossible to get part-time help now. "I'll have a talk with them, though," he said.

There was no trouble the next week, and my fears were allayed. On Saturday night, the young men asked if they could use the pickup to go to town. I gave them permission—Frank was up at the cow camp with

Lester, so we wouldn't be needing the truck. But I told the boys that they had to be home by nine o'clock. To my relief, they were home in time and remembered to thank me. I resumed my letter writing in the back dining room.

A half hour later I heard a noise at the gas storage tank. Someone was stealing gas. I turned off the kitchen lights and looked out the back door. The two young men were pushing the pickup away from the gas tank and into the lane heading for Dubois.

I was sure they had filled the tank in order to run off with the pickup. I phoned the local sheriff and told him about the theft. An hour later the sheriff brought the fellows back to the ranch. The older one apologized profusely and explained that he and his pal just wanted to hang around Dubois awhile and didn't think I would mind.

On Monday, I learned that the two fellows had each purchased a .22 caliber pistol on Saturday night. Now I was sure they were planning to leave. Fortunately, Frank and Lester came down from cow camp on Monday. Frank was alarmed after hearing about the gun purchases. He paid the young men and asked them to leave the next morning.

In November, a letter arrived for the younger one. The return address indicated it was from his mother. I debated whether to mark it "return to sender" or write to the woman, telling her that the boys had left six weeks before, that each had purchased a gun, and that they were heading for Los Angeles. I decided to write the letter.

Three weeks later, I received the woman's grateful reply. She wrote that against her and her husband's wishes, their son had run off with an older friend to see the "wild and woolly West." He contacted them only once since then, while he was at our ranch. When the parents received my letter, they called the Los Angeles Police Department, hopeful of locating their son. He was in jail, picked up for vagrancy. On arrival in L.A., the older "friend" had taken their son's money and his gun. The police released the boy when his parents sent a bus ticket for his return home.

Although we lived on the highway, we never locked our doors. I didn't feel threatened. I didn't want to be foolish, however, so whenever Frank was away, I slept with a .22 pistol.

Our bedroom was two steps above the other bedrooms. I discovered if I left the door partially ajar, I could see anyone coming up the stairs.

Once, Frank came home from cow camp a day early and found the .22 under his pillow. "What's this for?" he asked.

"I always keep it there while you're gone," I told him.

"This .22 wouldn't stop anyone! I'm going to get you a .45. If you ever have to use it, aim at your target's middle to be sure you hit him and stop the guy."

One Saturday night, I heard my cook come home from the dance and go to her room. Sometime later, I heard a noise on the stairs. I jumped out of bed, positioned myself at my bedroom door and, taking aim with the gun, demanded, "Who's there?"

A frightened voice said, "Don't shoot. Don't shoot! It's me! It's Alma!"

I had nearly shot our maid.

Frank and I were particularly pleased to have two extremely gentlemanly fellows working to help us complete our fall chores. We respected and trusted these older men, and they were always very polite and courteous to me. I attributed their excellent manners to their frontier upbringing at a time when women were scarce and their presence was revered.

That year, James was alone for the first time; all of his siblings were away at school. The evenings were long for him, so we permitted him to go to the bunkhouse to listen to the two old-timers reminisce about the pioneer days. One evening before James was ready to go to the bunkhouse, I asked him to do an errand for me. He squared his shoulders and declared, "You can't tell me what to do. You're only a woman!"

When Frank heard his son speak to me that way, he jumped up from his chair, placed his hands on James's shoulders, and said, "Don't you ever let me hear you say that again, or even think it! Your mother is a wonderful woman, and don't you ever forget it. Now do what she asked you to do."

While he scampered off to obey, Frank and I discussed the incident. We knew that James had fallen under the influence of the "gentlemen." Why, we wondered, were they antagonistic toward women? Then we realized the basis for their bitterness: Neither had achieved in life what he felt was his entitlement. They had to blame someone for their failures and evidently chose women. One man's wife had left him a long time before; the other man's wife probably should have.

We didn't want them to inculcate our young son with their philosophy. We forbade James to go to the bunkhouse again, and the men left when the fall harvest was done.

One summer, the Red Flat Association hired an old-timer, a settler with a wooden leg below his knee. The wooden leg was so uncomfortable that he did as little walking as possible. Whenever he stayed with us, he rode his horse from the bunkhouse to our house for meals—a distance of two hundred feet. His faithful companion was his horse, who tolerated his ineptness in mounting.

A number of years after he left the Red Flat Association, he was murdered on Little Warm Spring mountain. When the news reached Dubois, every available man became an amateur detective and rushed to the scene. The corpse had been found a hundred yards from his tethered horse. *Why had the old cowboy walked so far?* we wondered. *Or had he been shot on his horse, then fell off, and the criminal tied up the horse? What was the motive? Had he caught someone butchering a neighbor's beef? If so, where was the beef?*

The cowboy was quarrelsome but too lackadaisical to continue a feud. By the time eight or ten "detectives" tramped around the scene of the crime, no clues were left. The murderer could easily have been one of the investigators, adding fresh tracks to those he had previously made.

Who killed the cowboy? It is still an unsolved mystery.

10

OUR DOMESTIC HELP

THE BIZARRE INCIDENTS with our ranch help taught us a lot about human nature and kept us from boredom. My domestic help were as mercurial, inconsistent, and unpredictable as ranch crews. They were not, however, as great in number. The first few years, I was able to handle the cooking and cleaning and in so doing learned how to face emergencies, improvise, and be in charge. As the ranch developed, the family grew, and the number of summer guests increased. I needed help.

The year after the escalating feud between Mrs. Brown and Casey Jones, I had to find someone. A Dubois resident called me in the spring to ask me if I had hired a cook. If not, she said, her mother would like to spend the summer in Dubois and work in my kitchen. I hired the mother, whose pert appearance and pep belied her sixty years. She was an excellent cook. Her daily fresh-baked bread made a big hit with everyone. The kitchen was scrubbed every day. She attended every Saturday night dance, watching the dudes and local girls dance and sometimes joining them.

One Sunday morning she told me, "I'm quitting after breakfast."

I was shocked. She had seemed to be happy and enjoying all the praises for her cooking. It took me a moment to say, "Why? What has happened?"

"I danced with Jimmy Roosevelt last night!"

Evidently the honor of dancing with the President's son, who was a guest at the CM Dude Ranch, had elevated her self-esteem to a point where she felt she could no longer work as my cook.

My greatest pleasure was to hire young girls and train them to cook and manage a household. I taught four. They stayed with me until they got married. One of my girls, who had married a dairy farmer, came to see me a year after her marriage.

"I think of you every day when I handle our cream," she said. "Thank you for being cross with me when I didn't scrape yesterday's leftover cream can."

I smiled, remembering the incident well. After she had emptied the cream into the ten-gallon can where it was saved to make butter, I made her scrape out and measure the leftover cream, then multiply the amount by three hundred sixty-five. Finally we calculated its monetary value. If sold as sweet cream, what she had been wasting was the equivalent of a month's worth of groceries for two people.

Two weeks was the shortest time I kept a cook. The young girl seemed to be very attentive when I explained the routine, but evidently she never heard a word. On Monday, I showed her how to sort the clothes by color and amount of soil. Then I asked her to do the laundry while I prepared dinner. I looked out the window and saw pink and blotchy blue underwear on the line. When I asked her how it happened, she said the underwear load was small, so she dumped in the colored load and didn't think it would make any difference.

Thanksgiving Day fell during the girl's second—and last!—week of employment. Our family had been invited to the Knollenberg ranch for dinner. I woke up in the morning with a throbbing headache, and the movement of sheets set my nerves on edge. We could not cancel the dinner; our host's ranch was thirty-five miles away and they had no phone. We decided that Frank would take Ann, Carolyn, and Franklin to the Krollenbergs'. Helen and James would remain home to be looked after by my new help, while I stayed in bed.

In midafternoon, I was awakened. Squeals of laughter were coming from the playroom in the basement. I called to my cook. She did not answer. I struggled out of bed to locate her. She was sound asleep in her bedroom with the door closed. I woke her up and told her to come with me to the basement. Helen and James were skating on Ivory soap flakes, which they had scattered over the floor. My cook cleaned up the floor. I went back to bed, and she left Saturday morning.

The year we were feeding from sixteen to twenty-one people three times a day, I hired two women from Omaha. The younger one did the cooking, the older one assisted her and cleaned. The cook hated children, and we had five! The children were aware of her feelings, so they rarely ventured into the kitchen except for a glass of water.

One day Carolyn and Franklin went to the spring across the river, where they found a lot of small, harmless snakes. Franklin caught five of them and rushed home to show his treasure to me. As he went through the kitchen, he saw the cook and showed her his wriggly bouquet of snakes.

She shrieked, "Get out! Get out of here!"

Hearing the yelling, I ran to the kitchen. "What's happened?" I asked.

"That horrid little boy brought in a handful of snakes!"

"Where is he?"

"Outside."

I found Franklin and Carolyn. They were almost as frightened of the frantic cook as she had been of the snakes. I asked Franklin where the snakes were.

"They crawled under the tin can barrel. They won't hurt anybody."

Several days later, Carolyn was in the kitchen for a drink of water. The cook ordered her out, but my daughter continued drinking her water. The cook told her again to leave and kicked her in the shins.

No one's cooking was worth tolerating such behavior. The cook was off the ranch that day, which meant I had to take over meal planning. With the older woman's able assistance, I managed, but it was the longest, hardest summer I ever had.

All of my problems were solved when Greta came to stay. She could cook, she could clean, she loved our children, and best of all, she pampered me. She remained until it was time for Ann and Carolyn to learn to prepare meals and manage a household. Someone asked her if I had been difficult to work for. She said, "No. I always knew what she wanted, and she let me do it my own way and at my own pace."

11

HAVING BABIES

THE ANXIETY OF HAVING BABIES eighty miles from a doctor never abated. When I became pregnant with my second child in 1933, I chose a highly regarded physician in Riverton. I liked him and felt confident in his care. The whole county was shocked when this young man died of a heart attack. Forced to find another care giver, we chose the Carpenters' doctor in Lander. My first visit with him was two months before my due date. He insisted that I had miscalculated and that I was already in my eighth month. As a precaution, he wanted me to come to Lander two weeks before the baby was due.

I tried to convince the man that my date was correct. I was confident that my former doctor had also been correct.

The new physician then pointed out that February and March were our stormiest and coldest months, and I would find it traumatic to have a baby in a car under such circumstances. Neither Frank nor I wanted to undergo such an ordeal, so we acquiesced and made arrangements for me to stay in a huge, modern rooming and boardinghouse three blocks from Lander's Main Street. I had a large sunny room and bath upstairs.

I knew no one to visit or call on in Lander. I was there two weeks, which turned into three weeks, then six weeks.

The first week I spent in Lander passed quickly. I read *Anthony Adverse* and I walked for exercise. By the end of my first month in town, I had walked every street in Lander. I walked up and down Main Street every day, stopped in each store and business, and became acquainted with all the personnel. I strolled regularly through the lobby of the Noble Hotel, hoping that I'd see someone from Dubois using it as a meeting area. I went to the weekly change of the movie. I walked seven blocks to the library, borrowing only one book at a time so I would have an excuse to return. I finally begged my landlady to let me help her prepare the meals and set the table.

Frank came to see me once a week and brought Ann along. During this interminable wait, I was homesick, bored, and frustrated. I was angry with my doctor for having miscalculated my delivery. But whenever I seriously considered going home, I'd think about the horrors of having a baby born in a car in zero weather.

When I knew the baby was about to be born, I called the doctor, who arranged for a nurse to be with me. Next I called Frank, then my landlady took me to the hospital. Frank arrived an hour before Carolyn was born on March 23, 1934—one week past her original due date.

The Bishop Randall Hospital, where I stayed, was a twenty-bed facility. It was managed by a remarkable woman, Elizabeth Hainsworth. She not only officiated as manager, she was the anesthetist, the nursery supervisor, and meal planner. If there ever is a Hall of Fame for nurses, she should be in it.

Jean Brodie took care of me for the usual two-week stay. This merry, caring Scotswoman became one of my most treasured friends. She taught me how to make shortbread and to dance the highland fling. She would be with me during all my future stays and other family sojourns.

Franklin's arrival was in September of 1935. My new doctor, Dr. Holtz, advised me to come to Lander one week early. Although Franklin was a week late, time passed quickly, for this time I knew many people in town. When I felt it was time to leave for the hospital, I called Dr. Holtz. He took me to the hospital and stayed with me until Franklin was born. Jean Brodie was also in attendance.

After Frank received my call about my going to the hospital, he phoned a friend who wanted to visit his wife, who was also in the hospital. As they came around the curve at Diversion Dam, Frank ran into bands of sheep being driven to market. The animals covered the highway. He slammed on the brakes and drove slowly through the woolly beasts, scattering them everywhere but miraculously never hitting one.

When the men arrived in Lander, Main Street was filled with hundreds more of the woolly animals. As Frank slowed to detour down a side street, he remarked to his companion, "It's Friday the thirteenth. It's bound to be another girl."

When he arrived at the hospital, Jean Brodie met him and informed him, "Your Royal Highness has just been born."

During this stay in the hospital, I witnessed vicious prejudice. The nursery was a short distance down the hallway from our rooms, and we could clearly hear the nurses' conversations. The mother across the hall from me was a white woman married to an Indian. The nurses showed their disapproval of this by bathing her last, and she was the last to have her baby brought to her to nurse. Before the infant was taken to her, loud remarks were made: "Whose turn is it to take the half-breed?" "Look at the half-breed's hair standing on end." "How could a white woman ever marry an Indian?" "Does it make her a squaw?"

After the remarks were made, I could hear the mother crying. I told Jean Bradie to warn the nurses not to talk so loud, but they continued their cruel remarks.

On her third day, I heard the woman moving about in her room. Concerned, I went to her and asked if she needed help. She was dressed and had her bag packed. She told me she was leaving. She then went to the nursery, picked up her baby, walked down the stairs, and went out the front door. No one stopped her. All I could think was, *How cruel, how mean prejudice is!* All our souls came from the same source. Why should the color make a difference?

I worried about being able to take care of two babies seventeen months apart and not neglect Ann. She remained eager to try new activities, and I encouraged her to pursue them.

Franklin was a happy, contented baby. Carolyn showed her disapproval of the interloper by wetting her pants. When Franklin was six-months old, I heard him scream. I rushed to his crib and found that Carolyn had bitten one of his fingers to the bone. After being spanked, she must have decided he wouldn't go away, for the two children became inseparable. At this time I resolved to care for and teach our children and hire someone to do the cooking.

Two years later, I was preparing for our fourth child. We were building a new house, and, fascinated with its construction, I inspected its progress every day. Two days before I was to leave for Lander to await our baby's arrival, I fell over some lumber in the new house. The following afternoon, I knew the infant would soon be born. My greatest fear was that I would deliver it in the car.

Frank was stacking grain across the highway. I had to alert him to come home. I could have wrung the school bell, but we had designated that signal to mean a catastrophe. Some time before, I had figured out a way to signal: I remembered how Heidi yodeled in the Alps. We were in the mountains, so, I reasoned, why wouldn't it work here? After a bit of practice I could be heard a mile away.

I yodeled for Frank and waved a white tea towel. Whenever he heard my yodel, he would raise his hat to signal he had heard. We were on our way a half an hour after my first warning. My guardian angel took charge again. Helen wasn't born until after midnight, September 22, 1937.

James's arrival seventeen months later wasn't routine, either. I became huge and our friends predicted twins; but my doctor said no. As usual, I went to Lander a week before my due date. Evidently James hadn't read the calendar, for he still had not arrived a week after his date. Jean Brodie thought if I rode with her husband, Jack, in his pickup to his sheep ranch, the rough bouncing would encourage the baby to be born. I tried it, but nothing happened. A second trip didn't help, either.

When James finally arrived eleven days overdue, on March 9, 1939, he caused a stir in the hospital. He was twenty-three and three-quarters inches long—the longest baby ever born at Bishop Randall Hospital.

Having babies was not the only medical challenge presented to our family. When we arrived in the area, the mail came by rural delivery three times a week. A year later, we rented a box at the post office and received mail six days a week. The postal truck usually arrived at five o'clock. It was the time when many of us would do our shopping and visiting. I usually picked up the mail and always took Ann and Carolyn along. One summer afternoon, when Carolyn was twenty-six months old, the two girls went to the car to wait for me. In a few minutes I heard a scream. The back door of the car had slammed shut on the ring finger of Carolyn's left hand. I rushed to the car, picked up the shrieking child, and carried her to the kitchen and put her on the table. The end of her finger was hanging by a tiny bit of flesh, exposing the bone.

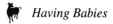

I carefully replaced the flesh over the bone and bandaged her hand so it couldn't be dislodged.

Frank was in the garage and had heard Carolyn's scream. When he saw the severity of her injury, he knew she would have to go to a doctor. He filled the car with gas while I got ready to go to Lander.

The doctor stitched her finger and advised me to leave her at the hospital, to be sure that the finger was healing properly and free of infection. I left her there and returned to the ranch.

Carolyn stayed three days and never missed us. She had the run of the hospital and charmed all the nurses, the doctors, and the kitchen help. Prior to letting her go home, the doctor strapped her hand to a light board to protect the sutured finger. Back at the ranch, Carolyn expected the same adulation and attention she had received in the hospital. Soon she was whacking us with her board when her wishes weren't granted. When we could no longer tolerate her behavior, I removed the board, and Carolyn quickly resumed her good-natured behavior.

12

THE WAR YEARS

ON THE SUNDAY AFTERNOON OF DECEMBER 7, 1941, the young children were playing with their toys, and the rest of us were absorbed in reading. We were interrupted at four o'clock with a phone call from a neighbor, who was a ham operator.

"Pearl Harbor was bombed!" he exclaimed.

Frank rushed to the radio to hear more about it, but he got nothing other than the usual daytime static. Sometimes we were able to get a faint reception on the car radio, so Frank and I raced to the garage and backed the car out into the yard. We heard only more static. We had to wait until sundown for more details.

The war years were harder to endure than the Depression. The young men in the reserves were called up immediately, including Dr. Holtz. By the fall of 1942, all the young men had been drafted or had enlisted. The older men left our area to work in lucrative jobs in war industries, and the women became Rosie the Riveters. Only a few older men stayed behind to help with ranch work.

Ranchers curtailed their farming for lack of irrigators and hay hands. Once again neighbors helped one another thresh grain, butcher, and brand. I was recruited at branding time to do the vaccinating. I learned how to inject the serum under the hide and not into the flesh. For my first few tries, I pinched the hide, and the serum squirted out the other side. Soon I mastered the technique, but I never liked doing it.

The biggest worry was to find chore boys or men during roundup time to feed the livestock and milk the cows. The first year, Frank found a midget who had groomed the famous racehorse Big Red. He spent the whole day currying Dolly and Dorcas. He braided their manes and tails. The horses never looked so sleek before or after he left.

The next year Frank found Roy, a small, forlorn, hungry sixteen-year-old. He was eager and willing to work. He proved himself so well that he later became the Red Flat cowboy on the mountain range.

Not only had the hay fields been neglected due to a lack of irrigators, but the potato patch suffered as well. We always raised enough potatoes for our winter supply. When it was time to harvest the crop, Frank recruited the whole family to help. The pickup was loaded with the children, potato sacks, and the potato digger. I drove the load to the patch. Frank rode Dolly, who was to pull the digger. Frank's role was to hold the digger in the ground, and I was to lead Dolly down the row. We had gone about twelve feet when the digger jumped out of the hard, dry ground. It caused Dolly to lunge forward and breathe down my neck.

Frank yelled at me, "Stop going so fast! I can't keep the digger in the ground."

"It's not my fault," I retorted. "Dolly goes faster only because you can't keep the digger in the ground."

"It's not my fault the ground is so hard. Let's try again."

After a few more unsuccessful attempts, Frank stopped. "I've had it!" he said. "I'm through."

The children picked up a half sack of potatoes, and we went home. We never planted potatoes again.

The only food problem we had was the rationing of sugar. We learned to give up sugar in coffee and tea in order to make more desserts—a necessary part of workers' meals, who needed it twice a day. I collected recipes substituting syrup and honey for sugar. Were they good? Suffice it to say that I never used them again after the war. I never wanted to eat any more peanut butter or canned peas, either. We had plenty of meat, though, and our Christmas gifts to our city relatives were much-appreciated hams or sides of bacon.

Ranchers and farmers had plenty of gasoline but were unable to buy new tires. Toward the end of the war, our family got "cabin fever." We planned a jaunt to visit friends who owned a ranch near Cora, Wyoming. We were only twenty miles from home when our jubilant mood was interrupted by a loud *thump, thump*. We had a flat tire. We looked at one another in disbelief. The children began to cry; I felt like crying but restrained myself. Frank changed the tire; but the spare was not in good shape, so we limped back to the ranch.

Whenever we bought a new tire, the worn one was put on a hay wagon or on field equipment. Frank examined all the tires and finally selected a fairly good one from a hay wagon. He put this on the car, and to everyone's relief and glee, we were off again to the Cora ranch.

There were no more Saturday night dances, no movies, and no radios. We needed to find entertainment. Someone learned about a square-dance caller in Jackson. We persuaded him to come to Dubois once a month to teach us the steps. Whenever he arrived, the grade-school gym was full of eager pupils awaiting him. The caller moved away, and another caller had to be found, for everyone enjoyed the dances too much to quit. A man from Cowheart was persuaded to try it. Records were acquired for the music, and we scheduled the dances every other week until the war was over.

Frank and I were one of eight couples who met once a month at one another's homes for a light supper. The evening was spent playing poker or bridge, square dancing, or playing games. We began at five and went home at nine, for we all had a lot of work to do the next day.

During the Depression and war years, our favorite entertainment for special guests was a trip to our cow camp. The two-room log cabin, home of the cowboy who herded for the Red Flat cattle, was positioned in front of a dense pine forest near a clear, cold, gurgling spring. Trout Creek flowed at the base of the mountain.

Our guests climbed into our pickup. Those riding in the back sat on blocks of rock salt covered with Navajo saddle blankets. At their feet was a box of food, utensils, fishing poles, and worms. Frank drove, and I sat in the back of the pickup. We sang as we bumped over the rutted roads and forded streams. Our destination was Trout Creek, full of pan-size fish. Frank was responsible for getting the fishermen organized. He preferred helping the children, who would squeal with glee when they hooked a fish. We needed only about a half hour to catch enough fish to satisfy everyone's appetite. My chore, meanwhile, was to gather wood and have a good fire ready on which to fry the fish. When the time came to go home, everyone was involved in putting out the camp-fire. We explained to them the dangers of a forest fire.

As the war continued, the cattle prices started to improve. Cattle breeders from the Midwest began coming west to buy directly from the ranchers. One young breeder knocked on our back door early one morning and asked for Frank. I told him Frank was rounding up cattle in the mountains. The young man asked me, "Would Mr. Mockler be interested in selling direct to me?"

"Yes. I'm sure he would. If you would like to see him, you could go with me to cow camp. I'm taking up supplies in a few minutes—just as soon as I finish packing."

He looked startled and said, "I'll go, but I'll drive my car."

"You'll never make it in your car," I told him. "You'll have to go with me. Come on in while I finish packing."

He stepped back, startled. "Oh, no, madam," he said. "I'll wait outside."

We took off, and after we forded the first stream, he said, "You were right. I wouldn't have had the nerve to cross that stream."

The breeder purchased the cattle. He was so pleased with the yearlings, he returned the next year to buy again. This time, he confessed why he was reluctant to come in our house the year before: He lived in an Amish community, and no man ever entered a house if the husband wasn't home. All conversations had to be in plain sight. No wonder he was taken aback by my forthrightness and boldness. I still surprise some people with my Western openness.

Not many were aware that a German prison camp was located in the mountains near Dubois. It was reached by an old logging road. The prisoners were delighted with their luck to be there. They were reluctant to go back to their war-torn country. Some planned to migrate to the United States. I wonder if any did.

13

PIONEERS OF THE WIND RIVER VALLEY

IF THE WAR HAD NOT BROKEN OUT, I might never have learned about the early settlers of our area. Our neighbor, Bill Burlingham, was a member of the first family that had come to the Wind River valley, in the fall of 1888. Bill often visited us, telling of his pioneer days. These stories piqued my interest and the desire to contact other pioneers. I began taking down their stories in their own words. I recently compiled all the oral histories and donated the manuscript to the Dubois Historical Society, which will print and distribute it so others can appreciate how much nerve, patience, ingenuity, and endurance it took to make the beautiful Wind River valley liveable.

Today, I believe we coddle, pamper, and protect our young adults, which deprives them of the thrill of testing their skills and talents. A synopsis of some of the early pioneers will give an idea of the hardships and the humor they found in their daily lives:

An entrepreneur sensed the potential of the Wind River valley, but the cowboy proved it was possible. Andrew Manseau, a French Canadian, was the first to explore every inch of the valley and the first to file a homestead in the area. His family had immigrated to Vermont from Canada when he was five years old. When he was eighteen, his restlessness took him through all the New England states and finally west. He stopped in Lander, where he had an uncle. The best job he could get was to cowboy for the ranchers in the Wind River mountains.

In the fall of 1889, he was living on his homestead when he suffered an accident. He told me:

> *I had a lot of horses to get rid of and corral for a buyer. One horse I wanted was particularly mean. I caught him by a rope and tethered him to a post. I told the man helping me to make the horse come closer so I could take up some slack on the rope. The horse made a run, and I caught my finger in the rope. It took all the flesh off of the bone. A neighbor dressed it. In three days, I had blood poisoning and had to be taken to the hospital in Fort Washakie. I was in the hospital six weeks. The doctor finally decided the finger had to come off. He put the finger in alcohol.*
>
> *While I was in the hospital, a guy called Old Whiskey Jack used to come around for a handout, becoming a big nuisance. One day someone thought of a good idea to get rid of him. They fixed up a big plate of fruit and put the finger near the bottom. He ate most of the fruit before he saw it. He moved it around and then picked it up. When he saw what it was, he let out a big yell, flew out of the door and over the hills. He never came back and went around saying the hospital cut up men and ate them. Everyone hearing the story laughed about it.*

Andy remembered well when the Burlinghams came to the valley in the fall of 1888. He said:

> *I had been riding in the hills all day. I saw some wagons coming up the road a way off. I waited to see who it was. I wondered who they could be. As they came closer, I counted seven children, a man, and a woman holding a baby in her arms. I thought, Who in the dickens would be coming up so late in the year? I felt sorry for the poor woman, who would be the only one here.*

The Burlinghams emigrated from Iowa. Over a number of years, they wandered their way west, finally getting to Fort Washakie. There, they stocked up on food and proceeded to the DuNoir River area. They crossed the rivers many times, each trip being more dangerous than the last. They crossed sagebrush flat on the DuNoir, where some squatters lived. They rented a small, one-room cabin. The door was so low, they had to stoop to enter.

Bill's sister Frances never forgot her first winter on the DuNoir. She told me:

> *It was awful being cooped up in the one little cabin. We kids were outside most of the time playing, fishing, and calling on*

A. M. Clark, another squatter who lived a mile away. Clark asked my sister Hattie and me to have Christmas dinner with him. We were to have elk steak, flapjacks, and prunes. Hattie and I talked about having prunes for days. Our supply of dried fruit was eaten long ago.

On the day before Christmas, it began to snow. It snowed all day and all night and got very cold. We couldn't go to Clark's home. We cried off and on all day.

Father spent the winter building a three-room house with a window in each room and a door into the kitchen. The window openings were covered with skins and the door with a tarpaulin. Father never got windows or doors for three years. The dirt floor was covered with a canvas. Beds were fastened to the wall, three in a row. They were made of small pine poles. Pine boughs were woven in and out and formed the base of the bed. They were covered with smaller branches. Mother had many downy quilts to go over them. They were very comfortable. The house was heated with a camp stove, the chimney going up and through the dirt roof. Mother cooked meals on that stove for many years.

My mother was usually cheerful, welcomed everyone, and was a favorite with all the bachelors and cowboys who enjoyed the fresh-baked bread that she always had to offer them.

Mother made all of our clothes by hand. Underwear was made of flour sacks that she bleached before she made the underwear. We girls had to learn how to sew. Our caps and mittens were knitted. The boys brought in the water for the wash, and we girls helped Mother wash. Our lights were "bitches"—a six-inch cloth an inch wide placed in a saucer of grease, usually bear grease, and then lit.

Bill remembered living near an Arapaho Indian camp:

They had a lot of kids, and we played with some of them even if we couldn't understand each other. We boys helped Mother with a garden she had planted a ways away from the house. One day she asked me to get some vegetables from the garden. When I got near the garden, a young Indian took a shot at me. It made me so mad, I ran to the house to get Father's gun. Father saw me and took the gun away from me. There is no doubt if I had killed an Indian, we would all be massacred.

We had a wonderful game that we played in the sagebrush. Each one of us stacked out a ranch. We built corrals and fences out of willows. We cut animals out of paper. We pretended we were herding cows and calves, and shot deer and elk.

None of us cared much for the shoes our father provided. He would skin out the hind legs of elk, leaving the heel. He turned them inside out and sewed up the bottoms. We hobbled around on them until the hide adapted to our feet. They were warm but got lousey. In the spring, we put our clothes and elk legs on ant heaps, and the ants cleaned the lice out in no time.

My father, Old John, was restless and a survivor. He never had much money. He was one of the best hunters and sold elk meat and hides. He liked his liquor and was often the life of a dance or saloon. He never bothered to file for a homestead. After living ten years as a squatter, someone filed on our place. Mother had filed a claim on Horse Creek, and we moved there.

In the early 1890s, homesteaders began staking out claims in the Dubois country. The Stringers were one family. The three eldest brothers came in the fall of 1899. When Asa saw the quaking aspen trees that had turned red and yellow just beyond our place, he thought of all the game that would be there. He learned about a forty-acre place that was going back to the government. Asa rode eighty miles on horseback to Lander to file on it. There, he learned that in order to file on a piece of land, the law said that one had to drive a team of horses across it. Asa hiked up to Dubois, borrowed a team of horses to cross the acreage, and hiked back to Lander, traveling three hundred and forty miles to get his claim of forty acres.

Six more Stringers arrived, including the mother, a sister, and four brothers. The horse that pulled their wagon from Arkansas died a few days after their arrival. They lived in cabins built on Asa's homestead. The older boys took any job they could find and pooled their money in order to live and improve their circumstances. Their diligence, standards, and successes irked other newcomers.

One enterprise was popular. They had a dance hall on a mesa about five miles above Dubois. One night a fight occurred that was later called "the Battle of San Juan Hill." The Stringers put out the word that John Burlingham, the favorite fiddler, would play for the April Fool's dance and the men must wear a coat. A coat? Hardly any man owned a decent coat to dance in. The coats they had were work coats, too heavy to wear indoors. A wool shirt and heavy pants were dress-up wear. The men were mad and decided it would be a good night for a fight and came prepared for one. Even the police officer came.

The festivities usually started around 9:30 P.M. and lasted until daylight. There were not many dances, so the revelers all made the most of the event. John Burlingham was late this night, but that was not unusual; he liked to make an entrance. The crowd was so large, extra benches had been brought out for additional seating. When John showed up drunk, he didn't see the bench across the door and fell headlong with his fiddle onto the middle of the dance floor.

The Burlinghams thought the Stringers had put the bench in front of the door on purpose to get even with John for coming late. When John landed on the floor, he got up ready to fight. Oscar Stringer jumped on him. When John's sons saw their father getting the worst of it, Tony, the youngest, picked up a piece of knotted wood and hit Oscar over the head.

Oscar fell backwards onto the bed of sleeping children. Babies began to bawl; mothers screamed at the men to quit. All the men got into the battle, which spilled outdoors. One man hit another over the head with a sock filled with washers that he had brought along for the fight. Finally, someone suggested that Carl Stringer and Bill Burlingham fight it out. After a number of punches, Bill was getting the better of Carl. Onlookers pulled them apart and stopped the fight.

The dances remained popular until a hall was built in the new town of Dubois, where it was more centrally located.

The Stringers exemplified many homesteaders who prospered through diligence and adherence to their standards. Out West it is called "lifting yourself by your own bootstraps."

The Weltys played a significant role in developing the Dubois country. The family arrived at Fort Washakie from Hamilton, Virginia. Dr. Welty had been sent by the government to be a physician to the Shoshone and Arapaho Indians. His son Frank's ambition was to go to West Point Academy. When that didn't materialize, Frank began exploring other lifestyles. He worked in the J. K. Moore Trading Post. He learned the Indian language, making him a valuable employee. This experience would one day prompt him to start his own store in Dubois.

He opened his first shop on his mother's homestead on Horse Creek. He was able to buy a store were Dubois is located now.

Frank Welty met everyone who came to the area. Owen Wister, who wrote *The Virginian,* was the most famous resident. He also knew all the ranchers in the area. One old-timer came to him and asked Frank to handle his money. Frank told me:

> *He couldn't read or write, and when a check was written,*
> *he would sign it with an X. When he needed money, he would*

draw it through me, and I kept the books for him. Soon there were too many ranchers coming to me to keep their money. In 1914, I decided to go into the banking business. I started the Dubois State Bank with a well-known banker, trusted by all who knew him. When he died, it was discovered that my partner had stolen forty thousand dollars. He had taken deposits and never recorded them. As an equal partner, I had to make up the difference.

Frank continued to improve his store and developed it into one of the finest western-goods outlets in the area.

In the early 1900s, a wave of homesteaders filed claims in the Dubois valley. George Cross's mother bought one in the fall of 1905. George said:

I came up in the spring with a bunch of cattle, to stay on the homestead. I was thirteen years old. I missed two years when I attended business school in Denver. In 1909, when I was fifteen, my mother paid me twenty dollars a month to stay on the place. That was the longest winter of my life. All I had were my dog and a horse. The snow was over two feet deep, so I couldn't go anywhere. I got so lonesome, I would go outside and look for anyone or any animal moving. I would strain to see smoke from a chimney four miles away.

That winter I made up my mind that I was going to own the outfit some day. When I came to the homestead, I had eighty-three dollars that I had earned herding sheep for Mother in Lander after school. I had five hundred dollars from my grandfather when he died. With this money, I bought some horses for five hundred seventy-five dollars. I broke them and made a good profit.

George kept his promise and bought his mother's homestead, enlarged it, and soon was recognized as the most astute rancher in the area. Like everyone else, he was willing to help when a disaster occurred. One of the worst catastrophes came in the summer of 1920. A cloudburst six miles up Horse Creek flooded Dubois. It destroyed a lot of property and took a number of lives. George told me:

I took my whole hay crew to town. We shoveled out the Welty Inn. The slush and mud were up to the piano keys. The sticky clay was hard to get off the shovels. The guys who died in the flood were laid out in the old Welty hall. A fellow who was sort of an undertaker took care of the bodies and put them on tables and covered them with sheets.

Pioneers of the Wind River Valley

One of the daytime caretakers moved one of the bodies into another room, and he then got on the table and pulled the sheet over him. The men in the saloon across the street were alerted to the prank. When the night crew came in, the man under the sheet moaned and drew up one leg a little. The four men were terrified and tried to get out of the door. The door opened to the inside. As soon as one got out, the door slammed shut. The men across the street roared with laughter.

George never stopped learning. With determination, grit, and ambition, he not only developed the best ranch on the DuNoir River, but he became the president of the Wyoming Senate. George's political position and enjoyment of public service proved to have an impact on Frank and my life, too.

14

LIBRARY WORK

FRANK AND I WORKED HARD, learning and perfecting the skills necessary to become good ranchers. I could cook at high altitudes on a wood and coal range and adequately feed hungry men. I refined my culinary skills by collecting gourmet recipes from the fabulous cooks in the area. Having unexpected company no longer flustered me, and I learned to extend meals in many devious ways. Our children no longer demanded constant attention.

I had reached a plateau. I needed a new challenge. I tried taking piano lessons but never got beyond playing hymns. When I attempted to sew, I became so frustrated that Frank asked me to quit. My knitting grew tighter with every row. I enjoyed collecting and classifying wildflowers, but that was only a hobby.

I needed something more demanding and meaningful. It came one evening in March of 1936. A whiskery neighbor came to the door and said, "I was wonderin' if you had somethin' to read."

"I think so," I told him. "What kind of books do you like?"

"Just anythin'. Just somethin' to read evenin's."

I showed him several books and magazines. He chose one of each. I told him, "When you finish these, bring them back and exchange them for more."

101

After the neighbor left, I picked up the books and magazines to take back to the living room. I stopped, suddenly remembering a vow I had made when I was eleven years old. I walked into the living room and said, "Frank, you know what I am going to do?"

"I have no idea."

"I'm going to start a library."

"You are?"

"Yes. I know just how that man felt without something to read."

When I was eleven years old, an epidemic of scarlet fever and diphtheria had swept through my country school. Several children died. Later there were isolated cases of scarlet fever. The school-board members came to the conclusion that the germs were harbored in books. As soon as school was out, all the books were burned and the schoolhouse was fumigated. I was devastated because during the summer months, children had always been allowed to borrow books. I now faced a summer of no reading.

My parents often went to Wisner on Saturdays to shop. When I went along, I usually played with Catherine, our doctor's daughter. One trip I lamented to her about the book burning and how I now had nothing to read. She suggested that I borrow materials from the Wisner library above the fire station. We went there, and I walked into a roomful of books. It took me a long time to choose the limit of three. I took them to the librarian, who sat behind a desk.

"What's your name?" she asked sternly.

"Esther Heyne."

"You are from the country. It will cost you a dollar to borrow books."

"A *dollar?*"

I never had more than a dime to spend when I went to town. It never occurred to me to ask my father for a whole dollar. Saddened, I returned the books to the shelves. On our way down the steep stairs I told Catherine, "When I get big, I'm going to see to it that no one ever has to pay to borrow a book."

I knew this was my opportunity to keep that promise.

During my waking hours, my mind churned with ideas about how to achieve my goal of a public library for Dubois. My first move was to test the idea with my friends. I was surprised and delighted with their enthusiastic responses.

I knew that in order to succeed, my goal had to be a community library and not *my* library. I asked Gladys Purdum if she would host a meeting at her home for those interested in establishing a library. Eleven women came. I was elected chairman of a committee of five to promote a campaign to further the idea of a library. We put an article in the local paper, inviting all who were interested in starting a library to come to a public meeting at the Community House. Twenty excited people came, eager and willing to work. Another story in the local paper asked everyone to donate books and leave them at stores and places of business.

Up and down Wind River, people found books in attics, basements, and their own libraries. It was a startling collection. Donated were ancient encyclopedias, two 1890 novels, mildewed books, torn books, and many new books. Almost nine-hundred books and forty dollars were collected.

Not everyone was enthusiastic, however, as indicated by their comments: "Kids will break out all the windows like they do at the school." "Who will use it?" "People don't know how to take care of books." "In a month the books will all be gone," and "Where's the money coming from?"

For a month the committee worked in our kitchen sorting and cataloguing the books.

While the project was getting under way, I had an occasion to go to Lander. I always called on Mr. Frankenfeldt (who had found the ranch for us). I told him about our library project. He informed me that he was on the Fremont County Library Board and that the board might be able to help us.

Mr. Frankenfeldt told me the history of Wyoming's library system: All of the counties had a Carnegie-endowed library supported with county funds. In 1921, Mr. Dobler, from Riverton—now a member of Fremont County's board—was instrumental in putting a law through the Wyoming legislature establishing the county branch system. This law made it possible for a county library board to assist branch libraries financially and loan books on a rotating basis. This unexpected assistance thrilled me so much, I would have hugged and kissed Mr. Frankenfeldt if he hadn't been so formal and reserved.

Before we could open, we had to find a place to house the books. The Community House would be too small. Putting the library inside the school would discourage adults from using it. Empty stores required too much rent. Finally, the Dubois Mercantile offered a one-room log cabin—free. It had been a rural schoolhouse before it was moved to

Dubois. The American Legion had used it before their permanent build-ing was erected. The forty dollars that had been donated repaired the broken windows and door and paid for shelving and a broom. We had no need for a dustpan; the cracks in the floor were so wide, debris could be swept through them. A chair, a table, a heater, and all the labor were donated.

The library opened in January of 1937 with six hundred eighty-eight volumes. Mrs. Rosebrook was the first librarian—unpaid. At first it was open only on Wednesdays and Saturdays. Children from the grade school two blocks away came on Wednesdays for their library day.

As soon as we were established, the county board gave us a new Encyclopedia Britannica and a large dictionary. It loaned us fifty books to be rotated every three months. After three months, it increased the loan to two hundred books, and the librarian received an hourly wage.

A local newspaper article in 1938 told of the success of the Dubois Community Library's first year:

Library Here Holds Open House Saturday

The Dubois Community Library held a successful open house Sunday, January 16, honoring its first year of active growth. Many old friends and some new ones came. Forty-four new books were received, including some that had been requested. The silver offering of four dollars is the nucleus of the new fund for the library. A year ago the library opened with seven hundred volumes. Today we own 1,727 volumes. Over 223 cards have been issued—115 to adults and 108 to children. The average number of books taken out in a month is 485. The last two months over eight hundred books have been taken out each month. Because we are a substation (branch) of the Fremont County Library, that library loans us two hundred books for a three-month period, exchanging these at the end of that time for two hundred more. They also subscribe to 19 magazines.

The librarian loved books and people. She was responsible for the library's congenial ambience for two years. When she moved away, we were fortunate, again, to have a librarian who had worked for four years in the Berea College Library in Kentucky—someone with technical training. She also proved her competence in handling emergencies. One day a cow walked through the open library door. The librarian calmly led her out.

The library grew so fast in its first three years that we had to find a larger facility. Instead of trying to locate another dilapidated building, I thought, why not build a new one? The idea was met with a lot of skepticism. The main concern was how to finance the project.

After considering all of our options, the board decided to build a library. One of the board members offered to draw up a plan. He did a lot of research on small libraries, their usage, and growth pattern. His plan was accepted and let out for bids. A log building would cost two hundred dollars less than a stone building. Some thought we should accept the low bid. I opted for a fireproof, stone building for two hundred dollars more. There was no consensus, so a vote was not taken.

Before the next meeting, I talked to all the board members individually and tried to persuade them of the merits of a stone building. I wasn't sure of the outcome of a vote so did not call for a vote and adjourned the meeting. After another month of conversations, I was finally confident a vote for a stone building would pass. It passed unanimously.

The building would cost $5,000. Plans were made to finance it. If it was to be a community library, ways had to be devised so everyone contributed, giving them a share in the project.

A list was made of all the families and businesses in the valley. Every board member took a list to contact. One man on my list wanted to donate a large sum. I asked him to give only half of it.

He was amazed. "I've often been asked to increase a donation, but never have I been asked to give less."

I explained to him that we wanted everyone to contribute. If he gave so much, others might feel they needn't give anything, and I wanted everyone to have a share in the library. He told me, "If you don't reach your goal, will you contact me?"

I assured him I would. (I did return several years later when the unique slab ceiling was installed by one of the last log craftsman in the area.)

Contributions were not only money. The sandstone cost nothing, and a trucker contributed his time, labor, and equipment to haul the sandstone to the building site. Carpenters donated all the labor. Home-talent plays and skit nights added to the building fund. Lander and Riverton businessmen also contributed. Donations ranged from fifty cents to five hundred dollars. All but two businesswomen gave something.

When the building was finished, everyone was invited for the laying of the cornerstone that held the list of all the donors. The Wyoming State librarian came from Cheyenne to dedicate the building.

The Dubois Community Library project caught the interest of many. Its story was written up in all the local and state papers. There was an article in the *Saturday Review of Literature*, where it was commented on by Katherine D. Patterson, from the Sullivan Memorial, Temple University, Philadelphia, Pennsylvania. She said, "I would like to borrow some of that Western enthusiasm for both our library patrons and staff."

John Underwood, a Dubois teacher and free-lance writer, wrote an article about the library and my role in starting it for the 1950 issue of *Household Magazine*. The article was reprinted in *Women's Magazine* issue in July 1951, and I was listed as Woman of the Month. It was reprinted in *Cow County,* the stock growers' magazine.

Because of my enthusiasm and interest in libraries, I was appointed to the County Library Board when the first vacancy occurred. In 1951, Governor Frank Barrett appointed me to the State Library and Historical Board. This group chose me to represent Wyoming on the National Trustee Board when Congress passed the Library Act. My first meeting was in Sacramento, California. The first distribution of funds was to be allocated to states on a population basis. When I asked what strings would be attached to receive the funds, the answer was "None."

I was not so naive that I accepted that, and the situation soon proved me right.

I became a member of the National Trustee Board and attended all the meetings. They were held in conjunction with the librarian meetings. In a few years, a strong movement was developing among librarians to upgrade all libraries by denying funds to facilities that did not employ a librarian with a degree in Library Science. The goal was admirable but proved devastating to hundreds of libraries, nearly all of them in Wyoming. Only a few universities in the West offered a library degree, so there was a dearth of librarians.

I attended a meeting in Omaha where the idea was presented. For two days I championed the plight of small libraries. Libraries were manned by local, dedicated people who always enjoyed a good rapport with the users. Not only rural libraries but many of the big city libraries could not profit by the restricted funds.

At the next national convention, I found an ally in the trustee delegate from Watts, California. Together we were able to scuttle the plan.

When I retired from my work as a library trustee, I had spent thirty-nine years fulfilling a vow I made when I was eleven years old.

15

OUR HOUSE

As soon as we moved onto our ranch, we had plans to build a new house someday. In 1937, the Depression was showing signs of abating, and prices were increasing. Frank reasoned that we should build our house then, even if it was sooner than originally contemplated. A lumberyard in Casper offered to build a two-bedroom house with a bath, living room, dining room, and kitchen anywhere in the state for $3,500. It was smaller than we needed, but we hoped to negotiate for a larger one. The lumber-yard couldn't meet our demands and suggested we hire an architect.

I had grandiose ideas about the new house we were going to have. I envisioned a U-shaped home with bedrooms in one wing, kitchen and dining room in another wing, and a large living room in between. The semiprotected area between the wings would be ideal for growing flowers. The plan proved too impractical, and the architect designed a two-story, ten-room house with a basement.

Bids were let out to a log builder and stone masons. To our amazement and delight, the stone masons' contractor's bid was lower. I had connived with the architect to build the range area of the kitchen to accommodate a propane-gas or electric stove. When Frank discovered there was no hole in the chimney for a stovepipe, he immediately ordered that one be made for a wood and coal range. Not wanting to contend with pockmarked linoleum, smoke, and ashes, I was devastated. I told Frank I didn't want the old range.

"I like to come home and, when it's cold, warm my cold feet on the oven door," he said. "It's part of living on a ranch."

He got his way; the range stayed until the oven door broke from having warmed so many feet.

Construction began in June. Our help dug the basement with a slip and a team of horses. Six feet below the surface, the remains of an open fire were unearthed, including charred wood and an oblong stone, which had a groove chiseled in the middle. I learned that this had been an old Indian weapon. A leather thong was tied in the groove, making it a lethal sling used to stun and kill game. Our son James still has that artifact. We dug around in the vicinity of the charred wood but found nothing else.

The position of the fire near the river, six feet below the surface, indicated that centuries of cloudbursts had washed soil from the eroding Red Hills.

The stone masons, Conrad and Phil Sundstrom, located yellow sandstone, which we hauled in our truck to the ranch. We built a ramp outside the structure, so the Sundstroms could affix the stones to its exterior. Conrad found an unusual, beautiful stone and placed it on the outside fireplace chimney. The morning after he had set it there, he realized that it dominated the chimney and replaced it. Only an artist with pride in his work would have bothered to do that.

The ramp tempted six-year-old Ann. Expending great effort, she pushed her tricycle to the top, got off and rested awhile, then mounted her three-wheeler for a ride down the slope. The men, seeing her speed down the incline, held their breath, fearing for her safety. When the little girl hit the ground, her tricycle bounced high in the air a couple of times, then landed upright with Ann still in the seat. She got off, shook herself, and looked around to see if anyone had witnessed her dangerous ride and might tattle to her parents.

Because of the Depression, we were able to hire two fine cabinetmakers. The quality of their carpentry was so precise and meticulous, I'm sure no corner could have been more than one-sixteenth of an inch off. All the woodwork was birch; all the doors were solid wood; the floors were oak. The Swede tie hacks, who cut the railroad ties for the Northwestern Railroad, hewed the huge beams by hand. The Sundstroms located a beautiful bluish stone aglitter with sparkling schist for the fireplace. It beckoned one to come near and share its warmth.

The first of December, Frank and I drove to Denver to buy rugs, draperies, and furniture for our new home. We asked the workmen not to use the fireplace because the damper was closed to prevent heat from going up the chimney. Unfortunately they disregarded our request, and rather than taking the odds and ends of debris to the gulch, the men decided to burn it in the fireplace. When Frank and I returned home, I wept when I saw the blackened stone. Muriatic acid had to be used to clean it, and the acid dissolved the sparkling schist completely.

We moved into our new home in February of 1938. Our family enjoyed the space of a ten-room house. The children had their own bedrooms. The hired men welcomed the shower we had installed in the basement for them.

One of the big thrills of having a new house was its central heating system, which would allow me to get rid of the wood and coal range. We all reveled in the heated bathrooms and the cozy warmth from the furnace and fireplace.

Frank needed a new challenge as much as I did. I found mine when I began the Dubois Community Library. Frank had none. He soon slipped into a behavior that almost destroyed our marriage. It began when an older friend picked him up one evening to join him for a drink at the Pine Tavern in Dubois. Soon the friend came several times a week, then every day.

Alarm bells went off in my head. I had no experience to cope with the problem. I didn't want to burden anyone with my concerns. I implored my guardian angel and Frank's to help us. No answer . . . or was there? After a year of Frank's excessive drinking, George Cross—aware of Frank's problem, as was everyone else in the valley—came to see us. George suggested we attend the Wyoming Stock Growers Convention in Gillette, Wyoming. Frank and I went and found the speeches enlightening and the camaraderie at luncheons and dinners fun. Frank was interested in the stock growers' goals, but it was only a temporary diversion.

While building our new house, he eased up on his nights in town but soon resumed his visits after we moved.

I knew I could never live with an alcoholic, and I feared that Frank would soon become one if he didn't quit. If I left him, how would I provide for four children under seven years of age? Besides, I loved him and wanted more for him and for all of us. I knew I could not confront him. We usually solved our differences with humor, but nothing I said or did reached him. Again I prayed for help. I continued to implore our guardian angels to rescue us. Finally help came during a heavy spring snowstorm that had not been predicted. Frank had gone out as usual.

After the children were in bed, I sat by the fire in the living room and agonized over our crisis. I felt so cornered and desperate, I finally gave in and cried until I ached. I fell asleep by the fire, unaware that it had begun to snow. Frank had not been dressed for the storm when he went out, and when his friend left him off at the gate, he stumbled and fell in the snow several times getting to our front door. Every time he fell, he knew he had to get up or freeze to death.

When he finally came inside, he saw me on the floor by the fire-place. He picked me up and saw that I had been crying. He held me tightly and groaned, "What am I doing? What have I done?"

He stopped his trips to Dubois that night.

The children were thrilled to have him back for storytelling and play after supper. We never discussed those painful years. There were no accusations voiced, no excuses, pains, or blames expressed. His actions atoned for his past conduct, as did my joy in knowing it was over.

16

NEW CHALLENGES

IN THE SPRING OF 1940, George Cross came with a suggestion, which he hoped Frank would be amenable to trying.

"I just learned that the Senate seat in Fremont County for the legislature is available. I'm thinking about running for it. If I do, would you be interested in running for my House seat? I think you're ready for a new challenge. How about it?"

Frank's eyes shone. The idea fascinated him. "You don't think I'm too young? I'm only thirty-one."

"Hell, no! It's ability that counts. I figure you have your ranch running in good order, and you'll have a lot in common with the legislators. Ranchers dominate both the House and Senate. The term comes at a time when it's easier for ranchers to be away than it is for businessmen. The legislature meets only every two years and lasts forty days. You can make it your vacation."

Frank turned to me. "I won't go unless you go with me. It will mean we'll be away from our children for quite a while."

"I want you to file," I said, seeing the excitement in his face. "We'll figure out a way to take care of our children."

Frank filed. It was a momentous decision—the beginning of a bright, exciting future filled with achievements. Campaigning required very little time or money. He had a few cards printed and ran a short advertisement in the local newspapers. We went to political rallies, and I was surprised that few women attended—this, in a state that had women's suffrage since 1890, when Wyoming entered the union.

Because of the poor reception on radio, we drove to Lander to get election returns for the primary. Several candidates were running for the available three House seats. We were nervous about Frank's youth and his being a relatively new resident of the county. His advantage was being a Republican in a Republican-dominated area. By ten o'clock, Frank and George had won handily. What a thrill! What excitement!

I was fortunate to have a good cook capable of looking after our children. During the forty-day session, I came home twice and stayed for a week. Frank and I resided at the Plains Hotel, the unofficial headquarters for all legislators. Lil Cross, George's wife, was my mentor. She went with me to bring my scanty wardrobe up to snuff. I joined four other women in a shopping trip to Denver. Some of the political functions were formal. I found a beautiful dusty-rose tulle and black-lace gown with a six-yard-wide skirt. I felt like Cinderella when Frank swept me around the dance floor.

Most of the legislators lived on the top floor of the Plains Hotel. The wives would get dressed in their robes and meet in someone's room every morning for coffee and chat. I didn't drink coffee but soon learned to like it, for I didn't want to miss the morning get-togethers.

Many of the Cheyenne organizations sponsored luncheons, programs, and entertainment for legislative wives. These affairs got us acquainted with the local citizens, and we began entertaining one another at luncheons, bridge parties and dinner-dances.

One afternoon, I lost my dignity! It happened during an era when everyone wore a hat. For daytime, the hats were elaborate, covered with flowers and feathers. In the evening, we wore them with a bunch of feathers perched on the front of our head. The only kind of hat I liked to wear was a Stetson or a cartwheel. For this particular luncheon affair, I found a blue-felt cartwheel hat with a veil and huge blue-chenille dots that complemented my new suit.

The attendance for the program was larger than anticipated, so extra chairs had to be brought into the room. Several of us, already seated, watched as the young waiters brought in additional chairs, holding them high overhead as they walked behind us. Suddenly my lovely new blue hat was going down the aisle, dangling on the leg of a chair! I was dumbfounded! I had to hurry after the waiter in pursuit of my hat. The

sight was so ridiculous and comical, I burst out laughing. So did all my friends who saw it happen. Whenever my friends looked at me during the program, wearing my retrieved blue cartwheel hat with big blue-chenille dots, they started laughing all over again.

I was intrigued by the making of laws and spent many hours observing the legislature in session. We were permitted to sit on the sidelines in the House and Senate. I listened to Frank, who became adept at succinctly summarizing a discussion and phrasing a motion to satisfy the majority. He soon became a leader and was elected Speaker of the House in 1950—the youngest ever to serve in that position.

When Frank became Speaker, he felt obligated to attend all lobbying group affairs and insisted I join him. One night, we were scheduled to attend a function where I would not know anyone. I didn't want to go, for I knew the women would be polite but reserved and noncommunicative. How would I "break the ice" and make them comfortable with me? I wondered. My dilemma was solved when I happened to walk past a trick shop the afternoon before the meeting. I saw a tulip attached to a long tube with a bulb on one end that, when pressed, would cause a worm to rise in the bloom. I owned a black dress that buttoned down the front and had a low neckline. I usually wore an artificial bouquet to camouflage the decolletage. I decided to wear the dress and place the tulip in my bouquet. I threaded the tube down the buttoned waist and under the belt with the bulb in a side pocket.

I arrived at the meeting and joined several women. My attempt to converse went as predicted. Responses were noncommittal until I pressed the bulb in my pocket. The first woman who saw the tulip and worm burst out laughing. Soon all the women saw it. Some brought their husbands to see it. All formality was forgotten, and I was warmly included in their conversations.

Frank was appointed to boards and committees because of his legislative and stock growers experiences and leadership. One important board was the Western Interstate Commission on Higher Education, nicknamed WICHE. It included most of the western states and Alaska and promoted arrangements with specialized schools—such as medical, veterinarian, dental, law, library, and engineering—so advanced-degree programs would be available, at no extra cost, to students whose home states couldn't afford to offer such education. I accompanied Frank to these meetings, paying my way but sharing his room for free.

Frank was appointed by our U.S. senator to serve on the National Land Law Review Committee—a conscientious, hardworking group. Wives were permitted to attend only once, when the board met in Montana.

Because I accompanied Frank so frequently, I became politically involved. One year I was one of two delegates representing Wyoming at the Women's National Republican meeting, but I had no desire to become involved on a national level.

Frank was Robert Taft's campaign manager for Wyoming. The Republican National Republican Convention, held in Chicago, was a sedate affair compared to the one I attended later as a delegate to the Goldwater Convention in San Francisco. To enter the hall, we had to go through a long line of angry protestors. I became tense and alert, but we were never threatened physically.

When Goldwater was nominated, the Rockefeller delegates from New York stalked out of the hall in front of the platform. Booing turned into a frenzied demonstration in support of Goldwater. I learned then how mobs were formed. A few zealots got the crowd yelling and moving. Soon everyone became involved. One had to join in or get trampled. Levelheaded leaders finally got the delegates and onlookers calmed so the convention could proceed.

Before Frank ended his legislative career, another event occurred that proved that politics could be unpredictable and illogical.

Frank succeeded in passing a law that prohibited the flaring of gas wells. The oil companies took out a full-page ad in the Lander and Riverton newspapers against Frank's role in this law. All the Fremont County voters were incensed at outsiders telling them how to vote. Frank was almost unanimously voted in to serve another four years.

The cool autumn evening and the warmth of the fireplace created a cozy atmosphere. I was curled up in my chair near the fireplace, absorbed in a detective story. Frank was in his large leather chair with his feet on the ottoman. He was resting his chin on his folded hands. He must have been watching me, for when I turned a page in my book he said, "Esther, I've been thinking."

I tensed immediately, for whenever he prefaced a thought with "I've been thinking...." I knew a critical decision had been made. I had no inkling what it could be, but his face told me it was serious.

"What is it?" I asked.

"I'm going to sell the ranch."

It took a moment for me to comprehend what he was telling me before I blurted out, "You are *what?*"

"All the pleasure of ranching is gone for me. My back pains me constantly. I can't ride a horse for very long, I can't plow the fields, I can't stack hay. And I don't want to be an armchair rancher!"

"What will you do if you sell the ranch?"

"I haven't decided."

"Would you like to own a business?"

"Not if I have to deal with labor. I'm too used to being boss. I couldn't take my help telling me what to do."

"What would you like me to do?"

"I can't think of a thing right now."

No one knew of Frank's decision while we both explored possibilities of another career. After attending the legislative session in 1956, I suddenly knew what Frank should do. He thoroughly enjoyed making laws, why not go to law school? The idea intrigued him. He had a reliable, able foreman who could run the ranch while he was in Laramie for the school terms.

He mulled the idea over for a year. In June of 1957, I suggested he enroll in the University of Wyoming Law School. He procrastinated until two weeks before school began. He would let fate decide for him. If he wasn't accepted because classes were full, then so be it. If he was accepted, then he had no choice but to go.

At forty-eight years of age, Frank went back to school. We had two weeks to rent a house and arrange for ranch operations to continue in our absence.

Once we had moved to Laramie, I had to figure out what to do with myself. When I had attended university to get my degree in education, there had been no time to enroll in art classes. *Why not enroll in one now?* I asked myself.

I chose a ceramics class under Bob Russin. My first project was to make a plaster of Paris mold for sculpturing. In my rush to get ready to carve, I removed the plaster of Paris from the mold too soon, and it sagged into a ham-shaped mound. Then I couldn't think of anything to carve. Mr. Russin suggested I "open it up." I dug a hole through the mound. Now it looked like a ham without a bone! My next try was to create a sleek, elegant Egyptian cat. It turned out to be a well-fed alley cat. One day Mr. Russin said to me, "I think you can make a better cake."

"I know I can," I told him. "I'll bring one for our weekly Friday treat."

I went home and made my favorite chocolate cake. It was the worst flop I had ever made. I put it down the garbage disposal and made another one.

Why was I experiencing all these failures? I wondered. Something was obviously wrong. I asked Frank what he thought the problem might be. He confided that he, too, had a problem. He understood everything he heard and read but couldn't remember to tell it back. We decided that for a very long time *we* had been in charge and had been the teachers; we were unaccustomed to being pupils. We were not listening or observing or being receptive to new directions. We returned to our classes on Monday, ready to begin our roles as pupils, and we successfully completed a year of schooling.

The following July I attended a meeting of my Library and Historical boards in Cheyenne. I told Frank that on my way home I would rent a place in Laramie for us, for his second semester.

"There isn't going to be another semester," he said. "I've decided it's a waste of time."

"If you don't go back, your friends will think you are a quitter."

"Then they will just have to think that."

"What is the real reason?" I asked him.

"I think I'm too old to compete with all the young people for a new practice when I finish."

"But you have experiences that they don't have to become a successful lawyer."

The more I thought about his not continuing, the surer I felt he must return. I stopped in Laramie on my way home from Cheyenne and rented a house and paid the first month's rent. I was apprehensive about telling Frank what I had done. I felt like a little kid confessing to a crime. When I told him, his answer was, "As long as you rented the house, I might as well go."

While we were in Laramie, Frank continued to serve in the Senate. The demands of law school made it impossible for him to do very much at-home campaigning when he was up for reelection, and his opponents took advantage of the situation. Ten days before election, we got a call at midnight from the Pecks, who owned the *Riverton Ranger*, urging him to come home immediately. The Democrats were crucifying him with lies and innuendos. One of the worst accusations was that he would fence the forest for the exclusive use of the cattlemen. It was a ludicrous claim; no individual nor the Wyoming Legislature had jurisdiction over federal lands.

Frank purchased radio time and angrily refuted all his opponents' lies. He won by a very narrow margin. I visited with some acquaintances after the election and asked why they would believe the ridiculous, out-of-character accusations. They said that because he didn't deny the charges, they thought they must be true. Ah! Politics! Not my cup of tea.

Frank enjoyed the give-and-take of the political arena, but I could never think of scathing or sharp retorts until I got home, so I learned to walk away from an argument.

17

EIGHTY MILES FROM A DOCTOR

How DOES ONE COPE with living eighty miles from a doctor and having to drive over a two-lane, rutted gravel road, going up and down steep hills and around treacherous hairpin curves, to reach him? You become innovative and you pray.

All I knew about health care was to be sanitary. No one warned me that the health and morale of a ranch would be my responsibility. Before we left for Wyoming, I was prudent enough to have stocked a medicine chest with aspirin, milk of magnesia, calamine lotion, mercurochrome, iodine, eucalyptus oil, peroxide, adhesive tapes, and a thermometer. At least we had a telephone to call a doctor for advice or an emergency.

My first panic occurred when Ann was twenty months old. She always took a nap after her noon meal. When she awakened, she would crawl out of her crib and join me in the kitchen or living room. One day she didn't appear at her usual time. Soon I became uneasy and went to her bedroom to check on her. She was awake. Her face was flushed, and when I picked her up, her little body was hot and limp. I took her temperature, and it was 103 degrees! I panicked.

We had no physician, so I called Carpenter's doctor. When he answered the phone, I was so frightened I was almost incoherent. He calmed me down and told me to find out if there was a contagious

119

children's disease that was epidemic in the area, then call him back. The only children Ann had been in contact with were a girl of four and her brother who was in the first grade. I called their mother, who informed me that chicken pox was making the rounds and she thought her son was coming down with it.

I notified the doctor, and he assumed that Ann would soon have chicken pox. I was to bathe her face and hands with cool water and give her lots of liquids to reduce her temperature. When the pustules formed, I should put mittens on her hands to prevent her from scratching the pustules and forming scars.

His diagnosis was correct, and I did as I had been instructed. Fortunately, the emergency soon passed. Ann recovered so quickly that she was well in three days.

I was relieved until another problem confronted me. While Frank and I were reading in the living room one night a week later, he complained, "Do you have to keep it so hot in here?"

"It's no warmer than usual," I replied. "You're just warm because of that heavy winter underwear you are wearing."

"I'm burning up. Feel me!"

He was hot and flushed. I checked his chest, and *he* had chicken pox! He was very ill for a week.

My first emergency occurred on a warm May day in 1933. Spring had come. The bluebirds had arrived and were flitting from tree to tree. The meadowlarks were singing in the pasture. The weather inspired the foreman's wife and me to rake and clean up our yards, which sloped to the river. Two-year-old Ann was in her sandbox discovering forgotten toys. Suddenly, a frantic call from the foreman's wife stopped my raking. I ran to where she had been working and found her on the ground.

"What happened?" I asked.

"I fell and ran a stick into my leg."

I gasped when I saw the ugly wound. It was five inches long and an inch deep. Blood and broken yellow fat cells were running down her leg. I could see bits of bark and dirt in the cut. The woman was heavy (a typical five-by-five woman), which made it difficult to get her onto her feet. I assisted her to her house, where I got a tub and put her foot in it. I gently poured warm water over the wound until it was washed clean of all blood, fat, and debris.

"I can't think of sewing the wound together," I told her. "I'll have to take you to Lander to a doctor."

"I am absolutely not going to a doctor! You'll have to do the best you can."

I was scared as I hurried to my house for medical supplies. How was I ever going to close such a deep cut? I began praying to my guardian angel for help. By the time I got to our medicine chest, I felt as if I had shifted into another gear and become very calm. I selected one-inch-wide adhesive tape, gauze packs, bandages, peroxide, mercurochrome, and scissors and went back to the injured woman with a plan in mind.

I sterilized the wound with peroxide, then thoroughly dried the cut with the gauze packs and poured mercurochrome on the wound. I cut the adhesive tape into one-eighth-inch strips and stretched them across the wound, leaving a space between the strips to allow for seepage. A light bandage protected the wound from contamination. When the cut healed, there was only a hairline scar. I would "stitch" many cuts using this method.

How did I know to do this? My theory is that all knowledge is out there to be tapped. By tuning in, it is received. New inventions come from complete absorption into this power when needed or understood.

A few months ago, I told my doctor about my experience. He congratulated me and said I had preceded his use of the butterfly bandage by two years.

When Frank's brother Dick and wife, Mildred, came for a visit in the summer of 1933, Mildred and I arranged to attend the World's Fair in Chicago in the fall. As soon as Frank took off on the cattle drive to Hudson, I left by car, with Ann, to spend several days with my parents in Wisner. Ann stayed in my mother's care, and I went to Omaha, where Mildred and I took the Union Pacific train to Chicago. We planned to return to Omaha when Frank's cattle train arrived.

We stayed at the Congress Hotel near the fairgrounds and explored every exhibit. The one that intrigued us the most was in a tent-like area with a number of chairs in it, where one could sit and rest weary feet. In front of the chairs was a table. On it was a large, thirty-inch box with a glass front that looked like a very fine meshed screen. Black, gray, or white dots projected an image—usually a face—onto the screen. The box was called "television."

The comments were fascinating: "There are always gimmicks at World Fairs." "It will never get off the ground." "Images are too vague." "Who would spend money on something like that?"

The next sequence of events almost cost me my life. On our train ride back to Omaha, I became ill with dysentery. I attributed it to the food we ate on the fairgrounds. By the time Frank, Ann, and I returned to the ranch, I was so exhausted I went to bed and stayed there.

At this time, Mrs. Anderson was working for me. She was very concerned about my weakness. On my second day at home, I thought I might feel better if I took a hot bath. On my way to the bathroom, I fainted. Mrs. Anderson picked me up and carried me to my bed. She said, "This is no ordinary dysentery. I'm going to call the doctor and have him send up some special medicine that I know will cure it."

The medicine that the doctor sent was Pepto Bismol! Mrs. Anderson was so incensed, she called the doctor immediately and told him she was a nurse. "I called you this morning to send some special medicine for Mrs. Mockler's dysentery and you sent me Pepto Bismol! Now you get off your butt and send me the medicine I asked for as fast as you can, or you will have one dead woman on your hands!"

I heard the conversation, but being dead didn't frighten me. Nor did the thought of missing Frank and Ann. All I wanted to do was float away.

The medicine that the doctor finally sent was for amoebic dysentery. Where had I contracted it? Several months later, we learned that the chef at the Congress Hotel, where we took our meals, was a carrier. Many had been infected, and some died. I recovered quickly with the medicine Mrs. Anderson wisely prescribed.

We can fly to the moon and film galaxies, but we can't cure a cold. I didn't invent a remedy, either, but I found a way to relieve the ailment. It was simple and only cost pennies. For small children, I used a large toilet-tissue box and cut a hole in one corner that was large enough to thread an electric cord through it. In a baby bottle warmer I placed a small glass with water and a teaspoon of eucalyptus oil. I placed the warmer in the box, threaded the cord through the hole, and plugged it into an electric outlet. I placed the child in the box and closed the lid. The child cried, forcing steam into the lungs. This treatment, a massage, and lots of liquid quickly cured the cold.

For older children and grownups, I cut a hole in a brown paper bag that was large enough to put a nose into. I placed the bag over a prepared bottle warmer. Deep breaths, along with a massage and liquids, eased the congestion.

One of the hired men got a chest cold and wanted me to make him a mustard plaster. I had never made one. All he could tell me was that it was a paste of mustard, flour, and water. I made some, spread it on an old cloth, covered it, and put it on the chest area. It brought relief. Why? I don't know, but it became the treatment for chest colds at our house.

The normal treatment for burns was to cover the area with Vaseline, but that often left rough scars. I read that tea was better for burns and left no ugly scars. This method was tested when Carolyn was two and a half. A visitor had taken an old teapot the children played with in their sandbox and filled it with boiling water to take to her cabin across the river. Carolyn saw the teapot on the table, reached for it, and sloshed boiling water on the inside of her upper arm. I dabbed a strong solution of tea on the burn. It relieved the pain and formed a thin coating over the burn. There was no scar when it healed.

I told Dr. Holtz of my discovery. He advised me to get tannic-acid powder, dilute it, and dot it on the burned areas. It was faster and readily available. Now I use aloe.

Dr. Holtz gave me another home remedy that is as effective, non-toxic, and inexpensive as anything known today: barley gruel for dysentery. I simmered pearl barley in a pot of water. When soft, I pureed it. To make it more palatable, I added a little vanilla. When the children drank a glass of it, they would always say, "Mommy, it feels so good." It checked the dysentery in a few hours.

Our numerous cats would sometimes get dysentery. I reasoned that if barley gruel cured our children's problem, why wouldn't it cure the cats? I made some for them. They lapped it up greedily, and their problem was cured, too.

Frank came into the house one morning, disturbed and worried. He said, "That young bull I just bought has a bad case of scours (dysentery). The medicine the vet gave me isn't curing it. I got to thinking that if barley cures our kids and the cats of dysentery, why wouldn't it cure my bull? Do you have some on hand?"

"I'm never without it."

"Let's give it a try."

I cooked up a box. Two hours after he gave the barley gruel to the bull, Frank reported that the barley was working and asked me to cook up another box of it. It cured the bull. I call it my "KCC cure"—kids, cats and cows!

Frank's first farming accident occurred at haying time in 1934. He always stacked the hay. He enjoyed forming the stack, and it gave him an overall view of the operation. By midafternoon, a stack needed one more load to top it out. The young man who sent the load up thought it would be funny to bring it up fast and dump the load on top of Frank before he could step aside. The load of hay came up too fast; it brushed Frank, and all the hay, off the stack. Frank fell off the twenty-foot stack and landed standing up. The pain in his lower back was so severe, he knew he had to go to a doctor. He told the hay hands to keep working, and he drove the truck to the house.

I started to get ready to take him to Lander but he insisted that he go alone in the truck. The doctor diagnosed his injury as a sprain and strapped it with wide adhesive tape. Ten years later, the injured area caused so much pain that he had to get relief. He went to an osteopath in Riverton. The doctor ran his fingers over the afflicted area and ordered Frank to go to an orthopedic surgeon in Casper. The surgeon discovered that Frank had three crushed vertebrae, caused by the fall from the haystack! Frank was fitted with a brace, which he used for the next forty years. The lingering effects of this injury would later force him to make a momentous decision that changed our lives.

His second accident, years later, was far more serious. The summer of 1951 was an exciting one for our family. Every member had a meaningful, responsible job—the first time all our children were involved in running the ranch. Ann, twenty, was our cook; Carolyn, seventeen, was the housekeeper; Franklin, sixteen, ran the hay forklift; and James, twelve, raked hay. Frank stacked the hay, and I was the general supervisor. The children were paid adult wages.

July 18 was a perfect day. Not a cloud drifted across the brilliant azure sky. Even the breeze was gentle and light. The hayfield would be stacked by supper time. The girls had everything under control for supper, so I had time to get the mail.

The last load of hay for the day was usually taken to the hay pens across the river. Franklin drove the tractor with the forklift, pulling Frank on top of a wagon load of hay. When they arrived, Frank got in the hay corral and waited for Franklin to dump a load of hay. On this particular day, not all the hay came off the fork so Franklin retripped it. Frank did not see him do it. Just as he began to spread the hay, the fork came down on him. The inch-wide prong knocked Frank's hat off, cut a four-inch gash on the back of his head, and slid down into his right shoulder at the neck. Blood pulsed from this wound. Franklin rushed to help his father.

"I think my jugular vein is cut," Frank told him. "Look at the blood spurt." He hunched his shoulder, and it stopped the spurting.

"Dad, lie down, and I'll get help."

"No, no. I'll go in the truck."

Ann and Carolyn, hearing the truck tear up to the back door, rushed outside. They knew something was seriously wrong.

"Dad's been hurt!" Franklin said. "Help me get him into the house."

While Ann washed the blood from his head and back, Frank continued to ask for me. He started to go upstairs just as I came home. The girls rushed to meet me and told me what had happened.

"Call Dr. Holtz," I told Ann. "Explain everything and say we'll meet him at his office as soon as possible."

I took the stairs two at a time, then stopped at the bedroom door to take a couple of calming breaths. As I walked into the room, Frank was struggling to put on a white shirt. When he saw me he said, "Help me get into this shirt. We've got to get to a doctor. I think I cut my jugular vein."

"I know. Ann is alerting Dr. Holtz right now. Let me look at your neck."

I saw no internal bleeding. His head wound exposed the bone. I cleaned it up and bandaged it. Frank was still dizzy and unsteady when I supported him going down the stairs. Franklin had the car gassed, and the girls had pillows and blankets for him to lie down in the back seat.

"I don't want him to lie down," I told them. "He has had a concussion, and it could be fatal."

I drove as fast as I dared. Or did I fly? I had to slow down in Dubois, for the street was full of jay-walking tourists. I wanted to yell, "Move, move!" No one had air conditioning, so everyone drove with the windows down. That was fortunate, for whenever I had to pass a car, I leaned on the horn, and the cars would move to the side of the road. I drove every inch of the bumpy road. I didn't want to start any bleeding.

When I slowed at Diversion Dam to make a right-hand turn onto pavement, Frank started to remove his head bandage with his left hand. "Honey, why are you doing that?" I asked.

"I don't want anyone in Lander to see me with my head all bandaged up."

"We are still thirty-five miles from Lander. Please leave it alone."

A few miles farther, I passed a patrolman. He blinked his lights but didn't follow me very long—he must have seen Frank's bandaged head. Frank remained very quiet the rest of the trip. I made the eighty miles in seventy-two minutes.

Dr. Holtz and two associates were waiting for me at his office. Dr. Holtz examined the wounds. "Take him to the hospital. We'll see you there right away."

The doctors steadied Frank and got him into the operating room. I waited outside where Jean Brodie was waiting for me. A half hour went by, and Frank was still in the operating room. I turned to Jean and said, "There must be something wrong. I can't stand it. Can you find out?"

"Everything will be all right," she assured me. "Don't worry. He's in good hands."

Finally Dr. Holtz came out to tell me what had happened. "We sat Frank on the operating table to examine the wounds. The one on his head seemed the most serious so we decided to attend to it first. When Frank lay facedown on the table, the cut in his neck pulsed blood all over. I asked for a bucket to catch it. His artery had been cut. What saved him was that a flap of the artery wall had fallen into the artery, and by shrugging his shoulder he was able to stop the flow. If the hayfork prong had gone in an eighth of an inch farther, it would have entered his lung, and no one could have saved him. He is a lucky man."

"Or he has a guardian angel who loves him," I said.

Frank stayed one night in the hospital. The next morning I said, "I'm so glad we can celebrate our anniversary today."

His eyes shone, and he said, "So am I. So am I."

We made other trips to the doctor and the hospital, but we had no more emergencies that I couldn't handle. Maybe my mother's litany of "Esther will do it" helped me innovate and believe I could respond to challenges when they occurred.

Living eighty miles from a doctor taught me several things: The first was to be calm and appear in charge. Faith and trust were half of the cure. Second, prayers put me in touch with knowledge "out there" when I was ready to receive it. Third, I learned that body is a marvelous creation, and with simple, cautious, caring respect for it, it can heal itself of most afflictions.

18

JAMES

ONE AFTERNOON in the summer of 1941, Ann, James, and I went to Dubois to get the mail. While there I heard the good news that we finally had a doctor in town. He was headquartered at the drugstore until he could find a suitable office.

On our way home, about a half a mile out of town, James opened the back door of the car. The wind pulled it back, and James tumbled out. I saw him fall and stopped immediately. Our little boy was rolling over and over, each time hitting his head on the pavement. When I picked him up, blood was flowing from the head wound, but he was still conscious. I thanked God for having a doctor in Dubois so I wouldn't have to drive to Lander. I only hoped he was still at the drugstore. He was.

The doctor took us to the back room, which was neat and clean. He examined the wriggling, crying boy's injury and told me, "I'll have to put him under to stitch the wound. I'll get the girl from the drugstore to help."

When she came in and heard what the doctor expected of her, she said, "I can't do that! I've never done it before."

The doctor told her, "It's easy. I'll show you how."

He got a gauze mask and opened a can of ether. Then he took the instruments from a bag and laid them on the counter.

"Don't you sterilize your instruments?" I asked.

127

"Of course." He got out a burner, some ether, and a pan, and began to light the burner.

I was alarmed. "You can't have a flame next to a can of ether!"

"You're right," he said sheepishly, and put the can of ether out the back door.

I thought, *This guy is no doctor; he's not even a good first-aid man.* I wanted to pick James up and leave. Then I thought, *His equipment is good. Maybe he's rattled because of James's screaming.* I let him proceed.

The doctor put James under. He cleaned the ragged cut and was about to take the first stitch. I suggested he cut the hair short around the abrasion. By the time he did that, James needed more ether. His nurse did it well. In a short time she said, "I have to quit. I'm going to pass out." She disappeared through the back door.

The doctor turned to me. "You take over."

"I can't! I'm afraid I'll give him too much."

"No, you won't. Give him only a few drops when he begins to move."

Soon *I* was woozy and had to go out the back door. The girl came back in to take my place. When the ordeal was over, I asked for the bill. He told me that James was his first patient, so his services were free.

That night James complained about his head aching. Thinking he had a mild concussion, I propped him up in bed. Neither of us got much sleep.

When morning came, Frank and I were still upset over the farcical medical treatment and thought we should take James to Dr. Holtz in Lander. Dr. Holtz was appalled by the puckered stitches. When he heard my story, he became angry and immediately called Denver to make inquiries about the doctor's credentials. There weren't any.

I asked Dr. Holtz if he could resuture the wound. He said the skin was too fragile to disturb. He gave James a tetanus shot. By the time James and I returned to Dubois at noon, the new doctor had disappeared.

We would have been better off going eighty miles to a doctor.

19

WOE

AN OMINOUS, ILL-STARRED, HEARTBREAKING YEAR began in 1941. In July, Ann attended a 4-H camp at the Tie Camp Headquarters in the mountains. We were unaware that someone at the camp had whooping cough until Ann came down with it a few days before we were to take our children to Lander for their shots. Because the children had already been exposed to the illness, the doctor wouldn't give them shots and eventually they all came down with it. Not until November did I get a full night's sleep.

After the holidays, all five children got the red measles. All the cases but Ann's were mild. She was very sick for two weeks. *Surely,* I thought, *we have had our share of childhood diseases!* I was wrong. In late April of 1942, the whole county was afflicted with a vicious flu virus that put adults as well as children to bed. Fortunately Ann, Carolyn, and Franklin had a mild case. The flu persisted, however, and minor epidemics occurred. James and Helen got sick in June.

James recovered quickly, but Helen showed signs of pneumonia. My home remedies weren't helping. We thought it best to take her to the hospital in Lander. Dr. Holtz, as well as a number of other doctors, had been recruited for military service. We went back to the doctor we first had. He put Helen in an oxygen tent. I stayed with her until I was sure that she was not frightened and was comfortable with the nurses.

129

I called the hospital at eight o'clock the next morning. The head nurse told me that Helen had been "out of her head" most of the night but was calm this morning. I asked, "What caused it?"

"I'd rather you asked the doctor," the nurse answered.

It sounded ominous to me, so I instructed the nurse to tell Helen I was coming to see her right away. When I met with the doctor, I asked him what had caused Helen's delirium.

"It's from the sulpha I gave her."

"You gave her sulpha?" I asked, alarmed. "Did you make the three tests recommended by the medical society?"

"No," he answered. "Those tests are just to make us old doctors feel obsolete. Your little girl is all right today. She has no fever, and you can take her home."

Helen was obviously over the flu. I decided that sulpha was truly a wonderful drug. She was still pale and tired but was soon playing with the other children. She began taking afternoon naps, however—uncommon for her. This concerned Frank and me so much that we decided to take Helen to another doctor in Lander, who prescribed vitamins and told us to come back in two weeks.

The vitamins didn't help. The doctor was concerned and advised us to go to a children's specialist in Denver. I agreed. He made the appointment immediately.

Our neighbor, Ethel, knew about Helen's illness. When I told her I was taking her to Denver, she said, "Go with me! I'm leaving for Denver tomorrow, and I don't like to drive alone."

After the pediatrician examined Helen in her office, she wanted her admitted to Children's Hospital for further tests. Whenever I asked the doctors what they thought her illness was, they said they wouldn't know until all the tests were completed. The serious looks on the doctors' faces worried me and activated my ulcer. The third day, I was told that our beautiful, intelligent little four-year-old had leukemia.

After I left the hospital, I walked the mile to Ethel's house like a robot, moving but not thinking. Ethel saw me coming and met me at the door. When I told her the devastating news, she said she would call her husband to tell Frank, who was at cow camp working cattle.

I went to my room and flung myself face down on the bed. All I did was say, "God help me! Help me!" After a while a comforting hand rested on my right shoulder. I looked up, thinking Ethel had come in. But no one was there.

Frank came to Denver the next day. When he met the doctor, he told her he would like to take Helen to the Mayo Clinic for a second opinion. She told us that the hospital was in constant touch with all hospitals on news about leukemia. Frank asked about blood transfusions. She recommended that Helen have one before we took her home. It would prolong her life a few weeks, but the pain in her bones would be unbearable. There was nothing we could do. Nothing!

After a week at home, Helen became too tired to play. Her bed was moved next to a window to our room, where she could watch all the ranch activities. We decided not to tell the other children that Helen wouldn't live. We wanted her last days to be as normal as possible.

James brought his toys and played with them beside her bed. Ann, Carolyn, and Franklin came to see her as soon as they arrived home from school. They took turns reading to her. When she napped, I would stand by her bed, memorizing her face. Her blond wavy hair caressing her brow . . . her long black eyelashes resting on her cheeks. She would open her blue eyes and reach for me to hug her. My tears flowed inside my body, crushing my heart. Other times I paced a five-by-seven-foot Persian rug. At night Frank and I would hold each other and agonize. I couldn't cry. I just felt stonier and stonier.

Helen turned five years old on September 22. Her bed was piled high with presents. Our family, several of our friends, and our help gathered to sing "Happy Birthday" and watch her blow out the candles. Helen took a bite of her cake and began opening gifts. She opened half of them and said, "I'm tired now. I'll open the rest tomorrow."

The next morning Helen didn't want her bath or massage. She didn't want to eat, and she slept all day. By evening, we sensed she was slipping away. Early the next morning, we were ready to take her to the hospital. Frank carried her downstairs to the kitchen where the children were waiting to say good-bye. They gave her a big hug and told her to hurry home.

Helen slept most of the time. When she awakened and saw us, she would say, "You are here."

We assured her we wouldn't leave. After midnight, September 24, she closed her blue eyes forever.

I remember participating in cremation arrangements, calling my mother, who came to be with us, and attending the funeral service. I do not recall the next three days except once when my mother said to me, "Esther, look to the hills whence cometh thy help."

I said, "But, Mama, I can't see the hills." The world had turned gray.

Frank was concerned by my lack of response to him, Mother, and the children. He finally suggested that Mother, James, and I join him to check on the fences on Pony Creek. As we came to a fence, I saw a gooseberry bush ablaze in orange and yellow leaves. I said, "Look at the gorgeous gooseberry bush."

It was the first color I had seen. When the children came home from school, they looked at me with anxious faces. I held out my arms to them. They rushed to me and hugged me. Their mother was back—yes, back from the abyss.

Days of "if only" plagued me. If only I had taken her to another doctor! If only she had not had sulpha! If only I had only treated her myself! All our dreams and plans for her were over.

Daily demands and our loving, caring friends assisted me back to reality. From that time on, material possessions lost all significance. Relationships were the only things that counted. It also taught me to live every day fully, for it could never return except in memory.

20

CHILDREN

DR. BENJAMIN SPOCK AND I would have had loud arguments about raising children. His philosophy of giving youngsters free rein to pursue their wants and interests produced a generation with no manners or consideration of others. The kindergarten teacher was forced to civilize them before they could listen and learn.

Frank and I believed that raising children would be the most important role we would ever assume, and we were committed to equipping them to become intelligent, contributing adults so this world would be a better place because they walked here. We believed that children were entrusted to their parents to love, nurture, and guide, with a few rules of conduct that allowed them the freedom to explore the world in safety. *Please, thank you, excuse me,* and *pardon me* were normal terms of respect.

Ranching is a dangerous occupation. We would have been foolhardy to allow our children to discover the perils by themselves. They had to be taught to be careful around the horses' and cows' heels, the bulls' horns, the swines' temper. They were shown the dangers of the cold, luring, rushing Wind River; the muddy, deep, feeder irrigation ditches; motorized machinery; and fire.

Routines began in the hospital nursery, where they were put on a feeding and sleeping schedule. When a baby got restless before feeding

133

time, the formula was increased and/or solid food was begun. Teatime came in midmorning. When the children began school, tea was served when they arrived home from school. Frank frequently joined the children and me to hear about their school activities.

There were regular times to go to bed, the hour depending on their age. They accepted the schedule and never felt banished if older siblings were allowed to stay up later. After supper Frank read to the children who were ready for bed until they could read to themselves. The older ones read or played. I notified them ten minutes before bedtime, giving them time to finish their reading or playing.

The one deviation occurred when James was two-and-a-half years old. He began a new habit, which baffled us. Possibly the hustle and bustle of the busy summer made him feel neglected. He went to bed at the regular time but, at eleven, would call, "Mama, Mama."

I went to his bedside and asked what he wanted. He had no problem, so I tucked him in, kissed him, and went to bed. He called again at two o'clock. He kept this up for three nights. On the fourth night I told Frank, "I'm exhausted from my broken sleep. There is nothing wrong with James."

"*I'll* go this time," he offered, and went into James' room. "What do you want?"

"I don't want you. I want Mama."

"Mama can't come."

James began to cry. Frank gave him a "spat." James went to sleep.

At two a.m., James called again. Frank repeated the procedure.

The second night was the same. The third night at eleven we heard James say "Ma—"He never finished the word. There was not another sound. Our bed shook with our laughter.

We had two dining rooms—one for the help, the other for the family and guests. We always took our evening meal together. Scoldings, reprimands, or complaints were taboo, and conversation was encouraged. The discussion could be philosophical, educational, entertaining, or a review of daily events. If a controversial statement was made, it had to be substantiated. This often meant a trip to the encyclopedia or dictionary. We never knew what mood would prevail. It was never boring.

Etiquette was taught at dinnertime. Franklin asked why it was so important. I told him someday he might be asked to a dinner at the governor's mansion. He would be so preoccupied wondering which fork to use, he would miss out on the interesting conversation around him.

All foods had to be tried. As soon as the children learned to serve themselves, they had to eat all they took. Once a child was excused from the table, he could not return.

The finest compliment about the children's behavior came when we took all five children—ages nine, six, five, three and one—on a road trip to California. A couple approached us in a restaurant after dinner and told us they had never observed a family so well mannered or having such a good time dining together.

Living on Highway 287, which was the road to Yellowstone National Park, made it easy for our friends to stop by for a visit. Our children were always welcome to greet them and stay as long as they were not bored. When very young, they didn't stay long. Franklin was four when he became fascinated with a tightly corsetted, large, elderly woman whose bosom dominated her figure. He stood beside her for a while staring at her bosom. Finally the lady said, "What do you want, little boy?"

Franklin pointed to her bosom and asked, "What have you got in there?"

We noticed that Helen was always the last one to greet the guests. She would stand in the doorway a few minutes before entering. Callers would say, "What a beautiful child!" or "Who is this pretty girl?"

One day Helen said to me, "I'm pretty, aren't I?"

At that moment I understood then why she made an entrance. I told her, "Yes, you are. You will stay that way if you are pretty inside."

Ann was three years older than Carolyn, so she amused herself by spending a great deal of her time roaming outdoors. To be able to find her easily, I bought her a red cap. I heard her calling me one day. I finally located the red cap in the midst of the woodpile. Ann had been climbing on it when a log rolled and trapped her in the middle of the pile of wood.

Another day I heard her call, " Mama, Mama!"

I located the red cap on top of the smokehouse. She couldn't get down. I helped her climb down. I made her go back up and remember where her foothold was going up, so she could use it coming down. I watched, as her little legs trembled reaching for the foothold. She got down without a mishap. I never had to rescue her again.

In spite of warnings about irrigation ditches, Ann, Carolyn, and Franklin all had to learn the hard way. A main feeder ditch was at the edge of our big lawn, near the highway. It went under our lane through a large culvert. The ditch was dry all winter. When water began to flow again in the spring, branches, weeds, and highway debris floated by. The three children went to the ditch to watch the debris. Suddenly, Franklin slipped on the wet bank and fell into the ditch. Ann raced to our lane, lay on her stomach, and caught Franklin by his coat as he was entering the debris-filled culvert. They came to the house to tell of their scare. I wondered how many traumas such as this I could survive.

The one underlying goal in teaching our children was that each one was responsible for his or her own actions. That put the onus on us to find ways to guide and teach. We started when they entered school.

As a member of our family, each child had one assigned chore to perform after school. In addition, the bed had to be made and pajamas put under the pillow. Ann and Carolyn had no problem remembering their duties of clearing the table and helping with the dishes.

Franklin's chores were to bring in wood for the kitchen stove, feed the chickens, and get the eggs. He performed well for a month; then the cook had to find him to bring in the wood and complete the rest of the responsibilities.

When I became aware of Franklin's forgetfulness, I had to find a way to put the onus on him to remember things. My method had to be pertinent, dramatic, and unforgettable.

He was surprised one day at school when he opened his lunch pail and found a piece of wood and an egg. He stared at it a moment, then muttered, "At least I have an egg." But when he cracked it, he saw it was a raw egg.

All the children laughed but immediately shared their lunch with him. (I had also put extra food in Ann's and Carolyn's pail.) When Franklin came home from school, he told me he had the best lunch he ever had. Days after the episode, he checked his lunch pail before he went to school. He never forgot his chores again.

An unusual and fascinating discovery was made shortly after Franklin entered school. He sometimes forgot to put his pajamas under his pillow. I warned him that if he continued, I would hide them, and he wouldn't be able to go to bed until he found them. The next time he forgot he said, "Now where did you hide my pajamas?" He thought a few minutes and walked directly to where they were hidden. He did it a second time, too. He had ESP.

Four years later, James inherited similar chores. He, too, soon forgot to feed the chickens and get the eggs. I needed to come up with another pertinent lesson. After several nights of reminding him, I waited until he was sound asleep. I went upstairs to waken him. I said, "James, you forgot to feed the chickens and get the eggs. I want you to get up and do it."

"Now?" he asked sleepily.

"Yes, now. Also leave the light on in the chicken house so the hens can see to eat. Otherwise they will quit laying." James grumbled as he put on his coat and overshoes. On his return, he stood in the living room door and proclaimed angrily, "I give you two weeks' notice, and I quit!" It took me a moment or two to come up with an answer. Then I said, "Well, James, I guess if you don't want to be a member of our family anymore, you will have to quit."

He was quiet for several moments in deep thought, then said, "I guess I'll be part of the family." He went upstairs to bed and never forgot his chores again.

When the children came home from school, they had to put their lunch pails on the kitchen counter. If they didn't, they were given no lunch the next day. No one forgot.

The other rule was that they had to hang up their wraps. If they didn't, I would throw their coats down the clothes chute. Carolyn was the worst offender. She was usually warned by her siblings to put her wrap away. One day no one reminded her. The next morning she looked everywhere for her coat. Suddenly she realized where it might be. She looked at me and wailed, "Mother, you didn't!"

I looked at her and said nothing.

Carolyn glared at me and yelled, "Mother, you did!" and raced down the basement stairs to retrieve her coat. She brought the garment up to show me. "Look at it! Look at it! It's all wrinkled!" She wore the coat to school.

Getting up in the morning was difficult for many, but I was not going to nag. I awakened every child individually, making certain each was up. I never called again. Whoever missed the school bus had to walk to school. I felt mean the one time that happened , but the strategy worked. There was no nagging, and the responsibility was where it belonged.

Our children, not meek and docile, sometimes needed a sharp reminder to behave. Instead of a switch or ruler, I used a butter paddle.

The miscreant had to go to the utensil drawer, get the butter paddle, hand it to me, bend over, and get a swat or two, depending on the seriousness of the crime. Franklin had deliberately broken a windowpane in the garage. He had to pay for a new pane and received two swats. On the second swat, the butter paddle broke. We all burst out laughing. After the children were grown, they told me that the worst part of the punishment was getting the paddle and having all the siblings witness their humiliation.

My father's insistence that his children "learn the value of the almighty dollar" left an impression on me, and I began training the children in the first grade. Every Monday they were given an allowance of five nickels: One nickel had to go to Sunday School; two nickels would take them to the weekly movie; that left two nickels to spend for an ice-cream cone, candy bar, package of gum, or a bag of peanuts or popcorn.

James was the only one who had a problem allocating his funds. The first day James received his five nickels, he took them to school and treated four of his friends and himself to ice cream cones. He had no money for the movie and had to stay home. He had no money for Sunday School, so he had to keep two nickels for the next week out of his next week's allowance, leaving just one nickel to buy a treat.

It was also my idea that the children save enough money for their senior year at the university. All but James had saved more than the $1,500 we were allowing them for a year. He had $500! He went, but to meet expenses, he drove trucks all over the country on weekends. At Christmas, he bought a chance on a $500 promotion and won. Two months before graduation, James reluctantly approached his father for a loan. Frank gave it to him with the stipulation that he pay it out of his wages when he graduated.

Our children benefited from learning social skills before they were fourteen years old. Dubois had no high school, so we knew we would have to send them away for that education. As soon as a child showed any interest in any activity in the house, I taught them about it. They all were interested in cooking and joined me in the kitchen on Monday mornings, while my help did the laundry, and all day Thursday, which was the cook's day off. As soon as the children could read recipes, they were permitted to go to the kitchen in the afternoon to cook or bake. All could prepare a meal by the time they reached high school.

One Thursday morning comes vividly to mind. Our kitchen was crowded. Ann was ten, Carolyn seven, Franklin six, Helen four, and James two. Helen and James were on the floor playing with pots and pans. Carolyn and Franklin were doing the dishes. Ann was peeling potatoes. When I finished making pies, I turned around and noticed James sitting in a glassy puddle and licking his fingers. He had upset a gallon of pure maple syrup, and the contents had gurgled onto the floor. His diaper was soaked with maple syrup. I plopped him into his high chair, where he licked his fingers while I cleaned up the precious sweetener.

We all remember being in the kitchen at Christmastime to bake German peppernuts, a small, hollow brown-sugar cookie. This traditional German recipe, over two hundred years old, was passed down through my mother's family. Everyone was given dough. The little ones usually ate theirs. The older children and Frank worked the dough until it was pliant enough to make three-fourth-inch rolls. I cut the rolls into three-fourth-inch pieces, then pinched them into a tepee shape. After they were baked, we all took a glass of milk, a spoon, and a big bowl of peppernuts to the table. We dropped several peppernuts into the milk. When they filled with milk and began to sink, they were retrieved with a spoon and popped into our mouths.

Frank taught the children to ride, fish, and shoot when they expressed an interest. At the age of three, Ann and James wanted to ride a horse. Carolyn and Franklin were five. They all learned to ride on the patient Danny.

Fishing was at our back door. It was a very rewarding sport. Three- and four-pound trout were easy to catch.

The children learned target shooting on our huge lawn. Besides aiming at a target, they had to learn how to carry a gun and locate other shooters and the dog. I was watching when Franklin had his first lesson. He handled the gun competently and aimed well but forgot about the dog. Just as he hit the target, he realized that the dog had run out ahead of him. As punishment, he wasn't allowed to participate in the next day's lesson; he had to watch. He joined the third lesson and observed every rule.

All learned to drive the car or tractor by the time they were twelve years old. They practiced in our yard and in the fields. They could drive on the highway when they were fourteen years old. Ann didn't care to wait. When she was thirteen and Frank and I were away, she decided to get the mail in the pickup. Carolyn and Franklin went along for the ride. Ann lost control of the truck when she went around a curve near Dubois, and the pickup landed on its roof. Franklin, who was riding in the back, jumped out and away from the truck. Carolyn couldn't, and crawled through the floorboards to get out. Ann slipped out her door. Several men saw the accident and put the pickup on its wheels, no worse for the upset.

Another near-fatal accident involved Franklin when he was ten years old. We were spending Thanksgiving Day with our neighbors. The children had an hour of play before dinner. Franklin was seated next to me at the dining room table. I noticed that his black, curly hair was wet at the back of his neck. I put my hand on it, and he grimaced. I asked, "How did you get your hair wet?"

Four pairs of eyes got big and round. No one answered. I asked again. The children told us that they had found an old dry well with a rope used to lower buckets. Franklin volunteered to hang on to the rope while it was lowered into the well. The rotten, frayed rope broke, and he plunged to the bottom and hit his head on a rock. I found a two-inch cut at the back of his head. He had a headache and lost his appetite, but the next day he was his usual busy self.

21

SCHOOLING WAS A HEADACHE

WE WERE WELL AWARE OF THE PROBLEMS of educating our children. The valley had three rural schools and the Dubois grade school. Two families were so far from any of those that they taught their children at home using the Calvert system, a correspondence course used by overseas army personnel and isolated families.

There was constant agitation from the Dubois grade school to consolidate all the schools. Our rural school district felt the Dubois district was more interested in the money that our taxes generated than in the needs of the students. The rural schools would not agree to consolidate unless Dubois agreed (1) to provide a bus service to the rural schools, and (2) to allow rural students to attend tuition free in the event that a high school was established. These terms were not met until 1948.

Ann had already graduated from our rural school. Carolyn went for seven years, Franklin six, and James one.

We provided books for our children as soon as they could hold one. Ann preferred books to dolls. She received several books on her fifth birthday. She chose one and took it to her father and announced, "I will read my new book for you."

"But you don't know how to read."

"Yes, I do," she said, and began to read.

Frank had assumed that when we had read to her from her old books, she had memorized the words.

When I learned that Ann could read, I contacted our friends who were using the Calvert system to find out if it had a kindergarten course. It did, and we enrolled Ann in it. She excelled in all the handcrafts, games, and some reading. She learned how to string beads, so, in the fall, we gathered wild rose hips for her to string. They were put on the Christmas tree. She has the string today, and it still has a fragrance.

I used the same course for Carolyn and Franklin. They usually preferred to create their own diversions. They eventually built a very long, low series of rooms along the river as their playhouse, using bits of lumber and tin from Frank's junk pile at the side of the blacksmith shed.

They found their recreation on the ranch and shared many good times with their school friends. Ann was the only one in her class. In order to provide her with a challenge, we enrolled her in the University of Nebraska extension course in typing. She completed with a high grade and earned two university credits.

So she could meet girls her age, I began a 4-H sewing course for all the girls in Dubois, and they exhibited their projects at the county fair. One category that was judged was "blind stitching." Several of the girls and Ann were considered for the blue ribbon. The judge came to me and said, "This blind stitch is perfect, but I can't see how it was done."

I showed her how I had taught the girls.

"I am going to disqualify all your girls," she said, "for none of the other contestants had a chance to do it that way!"

I objected to her illogic, but she was adamant, leaving me to placate my girls.

The following year, the 4-H club entered in the cooking division. Ann won a blue ribbon for her muffins.

Ann had to go to either Lander or Riverton for her high-school education. She would have to board and room with strangers, or we could rent a house in one of those towns and live there during the school year. Frank couldn't leave the ranch for months at a time, but his family was too dear to him to live away from them. The only alternative was a boarding school.

I sent for catalogues of Episcopal schools west of the Mississippi River. We found the perfect solution: It was St. Mary's for the girls and

Shattuck for the boys at Faribault, Minnesota. The schools were only a few blocks apart, making it possible to keep the siblings together.

It was difficult to have our children 1,150 miles away and miss out on their critical formative years. I tried to comfort myself by remembering that the English sent their children away at a much younger age and managed. Before our girls and boys graduated from college, they would have been away at school for nine years.

I usually took the children to Faribault. It was a two-day trip to Wisner, Nebraska, where my parents' home was. We visited them for one day before leaving for St. Mary's and Shattuck. I dreaded the return trip alone to Dubois. It was usually very hot; cars did not have air conditioning. I drank a lot of tea to keep awake.

By the time I reached Valentine, Nebraska, I was fighting sleep. I drove into the first gas station I saw. I asked the owner if I could take a nap under his large shade tree in the back of his station. He gave me permission. I drove under the tree, fell sideways in my seat, and slept for twenty minutes. I was refreshed enough to drive to Lusk. I filled the car with gas, and was soon on my way. Every year I stopped in Valentine. When the owner saw me, he would wave me to the tree for my nap.

We endured only two heart-stopping events while the children were at St. Mary's and Shattuck. In late fall of Franklin's senior year, I awoke in the middle of the night knowing he was in trouble. I told Frank, "Something is wrong with Franklin. I'm going to call the school."

"If something is wrong with Franklin, the school will contact us," he said. "I don't want you to call."

All day long I was receiving ESP messages from Franklin that he was sick. I was so distraught by suppertime that Frank let me call the school. Franklin was in the hospital at Minneapolis. As one of the captains in the Shattuck military program, he was put in charge of the homesick, runaway boys. The emotional strain and the flu exhausted him. The school had taken him to Minneapolis for tests. The doctors discovered he had crushed his skull on the Thanksgiving Day he fell in the well. The pressure on the pituitary gland had probably slowed his growth. The doctors asked Franklin if his mother had a record of his growth. He told them there was one on the basement door. I copied the record for the doctors, who told Franklin that they could remove the crushed skull area and put in a plate, and he would probably grow four more inches.

Franklin refused to take the risk, saying, "I can look my girl in the eyes now, and that's good enough for me."

The other episode occurred in James's first year at Shattuck. We were on our way home via Casper, Shoshone, and Riverton when an emergency call came to the ranch from Shattuck. Abe, our telephone operator, overheard the conversation. When we couldn't be reached, he volunteered to call the highway patrol and ask them to intercept us in Riverton. We were late and decided to take the shortcut around Riverton and missed the patrolman.

As soon as we got to the ranch, we were told to call Shattuck immediately. I wondered if my chest could contain my pounding heart. When we contacted the headmaster, he told us that James had a ruptured appendix, and the surgeons needed our permission to operate. Of course we gave it. I asked him what would have happened if he hadn't been able to contact us. He said, "What we're doing now—operating." The doctor had a hard time locating the ruptured appendix before they found it in the stomach area. James was a very sick boy and lucky to have avoided peritonitis.

There was one wonderful, lifetime benefit of being separated during the children's high school years—letter writing. Both schools demanded that their pupils write a letter home once a week. I wrote weekly with typed carbons so each child received one. A personal handwritten note was included for each, answering and counseling all personal concerns. Our letter writing continues to this day.

We extended the practice to include our grandchildren. When we lived too far away to choose appropriate gifts, we sent them a check instead...with one stipulation: A thank-you note was expected. If none came, there was no gift for the next event. The first letter we received from our grandson Bob said,

> Dear Mommo and Boppo,
>> Thank you for putting it in there.
>>> Love, Bob

Soon letters came between Christmas and birthdays. The first chronicled their activities. When they got to high school, they wrote about their problems. Frank and I answered the letters separately and never violated their confidences. I have saved all the letters to give to them someday. Now our great-grandchildren have begun writing.

A telephone call is intimate and personal, but a letter can be read and reread and enjoyed many times.

22

CHURCH WORK

THE FIRST BUILDING SEEN when coming around the bend into Dubois was the St. Thomas Episcopal church perched at the base of a steep hill. It was a prim, narrow, log building with a tall bell tower and the window frames and doors painted white. Inside were handmade wooden pews and kneeling benches for fifty parishioners and an old wheezy organ to accompany the singing.

Next door was a new log community house that had a large, cozy meeting room with a native stone fireplace, a kitchen, bedroom and bath. The Episcopal Guild raised funds to pay for its maintenance, augmented by plate offerings whenever services were held. St. Thomas was a missionary church and had no minister. Monthly services were provided by a priest from Ethete on the Indian Reservation sixty miles away. During the summer months, when dudes and tourists arrived, services were held every Sunday. If the minister gave good sermons, the fifty seats were filled.

When we arrived, the Episcopal United Thank Offering paid for two missionary workers—Miss Ross and Miss Jones, a nurse, who resided at the Community House. Miss Ross taught Sunday School, held a morning prayer service every Sunday, and called on all the families in the area. She was a tall, angular woman with a delightful sense of humor. Her good-hearted nature endeared her to everyone. She often commented

147

on her height. She went everywhere on a horse. She claimed that all she had to do to get off her horse was to stand up and let the horse ride out from under her.

Miss Jones was short and kept busy doing first aid. The two women were sometimes (lovingly) referred to as Mutt and Jeff.

Miss Ross and Miss Jones were some of our first dinner guests in 1932. I was pleased with my menu of fried spring chicken, our own garden vegetables of green beans, kohlrabi, head lettuce, and new potatoes, and fresh raspberry pie with whipped cream. I was unprepared for its results!

Why did I detect a taste of creosote with my first bite of the golden fried chicken? Then I remembered. When the chicken house was cleaned in the spring, the roosts had been painted with creosote to keep lice away. When Frank read the directions on the creosote can, it claimed results were surer if the chickens were dipped in a mild solution of creosote and water. I recalled how horrified I was to see the young fryers running around with wet feathers. I was sure they would all die. Fortunately, a warm sunny day prevented that catastrophe.

Frank, Miss Jones, and Miss Ross said they couldn't detect the creosote—even had second helpings.

My next shock came with my first mouthful of beans. I got a crunch, crunch of sand. My first reaction was to moan "it can't be," but I knew why. The previous day the man who irrigated our lawn flooded it, and the water ran into our well. We had to use river water until the well cleared. I did not know I should have used a sieve when washing beans. We laughed about the crunchy beans but didn't eat them. We laughed again when Miss Ross said, "I've never eaten creamed cucumbers, but these are delicious." The "cucumbers" were kohlrabi.

When I cleared the table, I said, "The whole dinner has been a disaster, but the dessert will make up for it." I went to the kitchen to whip the cream for the raspberry pie. The cream was too fresh and wouldn't whip. I quickly made a meringue, put it on the pie and into the oven to brown. When I opened the oven door, I gasped. The meringue had melted! The oven wasn't hot enough to brown it. I presented the servings to our guests saying, "You have had creosoted chicken, sandy beans, and creamed cucumbers and now I present you with topless raspberry pie." We laughed until tears rolled down our cheeks.

Miss Ross noticed our piano and asked me if I would play for the morning prayer service. I said that I would. I had to play on the old organ that was also very temperamental. Sometimes the left pedal would collapse with a thump, and there would be no musical sound. The congregation was startled to hear no music and see no organist. I had dropped out of sight to get on my hands and knees to repair the pedal. The congregation kept on singing. If I was lucky in repairing the pedal, I appeared again in time to play the Amen.

The Depression dried up the United Thank Offering funds, forcing Miss Ross and Miss Jones to leave. Services were again held once a month, provided by the Ethete priest from the Indian Reservation. A Dubois favorite was Dr. Tyler, a retired minister from a large church on the East Coast, who had become bored with retirement and decided to do missionary work. His sermons were so outstanding that our little church was crowded. I've always remembered one sermon about a sign he had seen in England that said, "Be a little kinder than is necessary." He also shared with us the secret of giving a good sermon or a good speech. It was, "State your point. Give three illustrations to prove it, and finish in ten minutes."

Dr. Tyler liked to hunt. Frank took him every fall he was here. He would come dressed for hunting when he arrived for the service—his robe never covered his cowboy boots.

After the war, big city churches in the Midwest and the East would arrange for ministers to spend one or two months' vacation in Dubois and provide the services. The first family to come was Joe Minnis, his wife, Katherine, and their four children from Trinity Church in New York City. Two of their children were Carolyn's and Franklin's age, and they came almost every day to play. Our children took them to all their favorite haunts on the ranch. One that intrigued our children this summer was to climb in the Red Hills where Carolyn and Franklin got a thrill crawling out to a very narrow ridge and straddling it. One of the Minnis boys tried and became frightened when he began to back off. He said, "If I get killed, my father will sue you!"

At the dinner table that night, Franklin asked his father, "What does 'sue' mean?"

Frank said, "It could mean an Indian, or a lawsuit. Why do you ask?"

Franklin recounted the incident. After Frank's explanation, they never took the Minnis boys to the Red Hills again.

Several years later, the Kenneth Gass family arrived from Massilon, Ohio. They enjoyed our valley so much they spent many summers there.

One year we took the Gass family and our family on a pack trip to Ross Lake to fish. Kenneth held a communion service one morning as the sun came up, bathing the mountains and the lake in a rosy glow. The altar was a fallen log. Our choir was singing birds. None of us have forgotten the experience nor have I ever had one more meaningful.

The most outstanding service in our little church was conducted by the Archbishop of Canterbury of England, who was a guest at the Brooks Lake Lodge dude ranch. He wore his robes and miter. His robes filled the aisle and the altar area. We were all so in awe of the splendor that I doubt if anyone heard his message.

23

THE EPISCOPAL GUILD

WHEN WE MOVED TO DUBOIS, the Episcopal Guild was the only women's organization in the area, and it welcomed members of all faiths. Socializing at the monthly meetings and be entertained by stimulating programs were pleasant activities. The guild's only money-making project was a bazaar and bake sale. It did not generate much income—about sixty dollars a year—and with the guild's desire to provide new services, we realized a need to attract outside money.

The wife of the Wyoming Tie and Timber Company owner suggested hosting a Swedish smorgasbord, offering many of the dishes she had learned from the Swedes who moved to America to cut railroad ties. Over a hundred diners came to the first dinner to savor lox, meatballs, fish balls, ham, herring salad, lingonberries, hardtack, *fatigman, kram* (a fruit dessert), homemade breads, and coffee cakes. All Swedish foods were purchased from a specialty wholesale house in Chicago. Word of the authenticity of the well-prepared cuisine lured three hundred diners to participate the next year. Soon reservations were being made for 1,500 for three seatings.

A rummage sale, which proved to be another lucrative fund-raiser, was proposed by the owner of the T Cross dude ranch. The first event was held in an empty building on Main Street. For that sale, I was one of many to help arrange the donations and the last one to leave and lock the store. When I stepped out the door, Oscar Stringer, my postmaster friend, was waiting for me. He said, "I want to buy that globe in the window now."

"Oscar," I told him, "we have a rule that no one can make a purchase until the sale begins tomorrow at nine o'clock."

"But I've got to work and can't get here then. If I give you the dollar now, will you buy it for me tomorrow?"

"Sure, I'd be glad to do that."

While I stood there, Oscar unbuttoned his trousers and slid them down to his knees. He reached into a second pair of trousers for his pocketbook, then drew out a long leather bag, unfastened the clasp, took out a silver dollar, and handed it to me.

I stood there paralyzed, looking up and down Main Street, praying that no one saw me with the half-dressed Oscar. He pulled up his trousers and walked away, happy to have a globe. *This will seem funny to me tomorrow,* I thought, still horrified.

A rummage sale was a new experience for me. The fabulous bargains astounded me and helped me appreciate Frank's fascination with pawn shops. By the time it was my turn to chair our rummage sale it was called The Opportunity Sale, and I had learned of another innovation. It was risky, but the Dubois women were amenable to taking risks. All merchandise in the first morning of the sale would be sold for 150 percent of the marked price. In the afternoon, it would sell for the marked price. The next morning it was reduced to half price. The experiment was a tremendous success. By noon, most of the merchandise had been sold. By noon of the second day, only a full toilet-tissue box was left, and this was donated to the reservation.

Although Dubois had a seasonal influx of tourists, the tiny town had no gift shop. The dude ranchers were forced to stock Indian jewelry, beadwork, and Western items, which they sold on consignment to their guests.

A dude rancher brought a suitcase of consigned gifts to a guild meeting and offered it to the members, with the profit going to the guild. One could almost hear the wheels turning in every head in the room: *Why don't we start a gift shop?* The Corral came into existence that day.

We needed over a year to get it established. Someone donated a lot on the west end of Dubois. We donated a log cabin, which was hauled free of charge to the spot by a trucker. My lawyer friend in Lander drew up papers permitting the guild to make sales without collecting tax. A guild representative traveled to the annual Denver gift show to purchase the shop's inventory. We arranged consignments for expensive jewelry and scheduled the volunteer staffers. It was the toughest, most involved project we had ever undertaken. When established, however, its profits made it a viable enterprise.

When I was elected president of our guild, I wanted to learn about the church work in our diocese. *What better way,* I thought, *than to attend the state convention?* To my surprise, I was appointed to a committee. It led to more involvement, and I was elected president of the state Episcopal churchwomen in 1951–1953. This position came at an opportune time: Our youngest son, James, had entered Shattuck Academy at Faribault, Minnesota, and I needed some activity to help me adjust to my empty nest. I decided to visit all the guilds in the state. It had never been done, and the idea was met with surprise and approval. I learned that many of the individual groups were not aware of the services the state could provide. I inaugurated a state handbook, with pertinent information in a loose-leaf notebook, so updating would be easy. The handbook is still in use.

After my term was over, I thought of the quote "The king is dead. Long live the king." How does one avoid the feeling of being put aside? How does one avoid grieving the past? My way has been to become completely involved with the present moment or phase, so there are no regrets about moving forward into a new adventure.

24

FATE STEPS IN

FRANK'S MISGIVINGS ABOUT HIS DECISION to attend law school weren't over when he graduated. He was *not* going to take the bar exam. When I asked why, he said, "What if I don't pass?"

"You'll take it again, like many do."

When he kept insisting that he wasn't going to take the exam, I was so sure he should and would pass it that I contacted a number of his lawyer friends to pressure him to take the test. Bless them all, for they convinced him to sit for the exam, and he passed.

Soon after, his good friend Jack Crofts asked him to join his firm in Lander.

The day arrived when we packed up to leave for our new home and a new lifestyle in Lander. Had it really been twenty-nine years since this young blond, blue-eyed, eager girl with a healthy baby girl in her arms and an excited husband arrived on a ranch in Wyoming?

I knew I would always remember the thrill of seeing our first home, a long, log house with hop vines covering one end, nestled in front of trees with a rushing river behind it, surrounded with spectacular scenery that would inspire me every day.

As I packed the supplies from the medicine cabinet, numerous first-aid episodes flashed by: the day when I had to stitch a deep, five-inch cut and my guardian angel helped me to devise a version of the butter-fly bandage two years before it was marketed. . . of the many trips to Lander . . . the unlicensed "doctor" who stitched James's head wound. . . . The worst experience, both emotionally and in terms of danger, was when Frank's life hung in the balance.

I stopped a moment to agonize again over the loss of our beautiful Helen.

The living room seemed to echo with the laughter and fun we had before a cozy fireplace. The kitchen brought to mind the Christmases we spent there, with the whole family making peppernuts. The vision reminded me of wintertime, when cold feet were warmed on the open door of the wood and coal range, and the smell of wet, wool socks and mittens drying wafted across the room.

I realized how fortunate I was to have had the opportunity to learn about human nature with the numerous helpers we had over the twenty-nine years. I would never forget the irresponsible teenagers' shooting in the bunkhouse and sending a bullet through the living room window, just missing James and terrifying both of us.

I would surely miss the warm summer days when we took our family and guests to picnic and fish.

I tried to live each day fully, so I had many memories to take with me. I vowed to continue my one habit of waking up in the morning, saying my prayers, and wondering with optimism and eager anticipation what the day has in store for me.

EPILOGUE

MY ADVENTURES DID NOT END when we moved to Lander, Wyoming. After having been Frank's partner for thirty years I was apprehensive about being a lawyer's wife, where I would be excluded from his daily work. I needed a new challenge and again, my guardian angel came to my rescue.

A month before we moved to Lander we drove there to find a place to live. Soon we located a nice four bedroom house on Main Street. After the deal was made I went to a nearby beauty parlor for a shampoo and set. Shortly after I had been seated another woman entered and was soon introduced to me as Dottie, a co-owner of the local radio station, KOVE. After we had chatted for a while she informed me that KOVE needed a new announcer for the "Listen Ladies" program. Noticing my look of astonishment she said, "It's a fifteen minute program, five days of the week at nine in the morning."

After I recovered from the surprise of the unexpected offer, I said, "I don't know what the program is about."

Dotty said, "You will report the births, deaths, and weddings, give a recipe and three ads."

"I have never been on the radio, maybe my voice will not project."

"I am a good judge of that and I know your's will. Why don't you stop at the studio on your way home. We will make a test, acquaint you with the procedure, and you'll see how easy it will be."

Frank was pleased with my new adventure, and I accepted the job.

Finding the recipes was easy. My concern was my delivery. I asked my friends and my daughter living in Riverton to critique my program. At the end of the week they all had the same criticism: I spoke too fast.

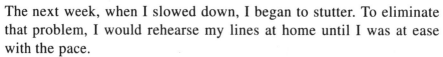

The next week, when I slowed down, I began to stutter. To eliminate that problem, I would rehearse my lines at home until I was at ease with the pace.

Soon I dropped the notices of the births, deaths and weddings. Lander and all the surrounding areas were homes of many many old timers, and I began interviewing them and some of the Indians at the nearby Fort Washaie Reservation. The new format was so well received that I began doing all the interviews of the dignitaries who came to town including governors, congressmen, bishops, even the entertainers who came for the annual One Shot Antelope Hunt.

I left the program after five enjoyable years in order to able to go with Frank to his many hearings in Washington, D.C., and his national board meetings. I had also been appointed to a national Board of Trustees that involved a great deal of travel. And I wanted to devote more time with my new hobby of making pottery on the wheel.

After ten years of law practice Frank said to me one day, "I have been thinking that I would like to do something for my country overseas. What do you think of that?"

"I think it would be exciting. What do you have in mind?"

"Maybe somewhere in Mexico or South America. We both speak Spanish and that should be a plus."

On a trip to Cheyenne to prepare to go to Washington, D.C., for a hearing, Frank confided his ambition to Governor Stan Hathaway. Stan was excited about it and immediately called the State Department to make an appointment for Frank after the hearing. While at the meeting he learned there was nothing available in the State Department, but something was coming up in Interior. At this interview he was questioned about his hobbies and lifestyle for forty-five minutes.

He arrived home on a Friday and on Monday he received word from the Department of Interior that he was to get his resume in immediately for an appointment that was going to be made on the following Friday.

On Friday we heard nothing. No news on Saturday. Then on Sunday the phone rang at seven o'clock. Our senator and good friend, Cliff Hansen, told Frank that the Governor of Samoa would call in an hour and ask him to be his Lieutenant Governor. Samoa was not unknown to us. A law school classmate of Frank had spent several years in Samoa as treasurer. One evening he had invited his classmates and their spouses to view his slides and to hear him tell of his years there as treasurer. We knew it was tropical, below the equator and that it was hot and humid.

Frank was worried about my intolerance of high temperatures and asked me if I thought I could stand it. I told him they had electricity and we could take along air conditioners. When the phone rang at seven-thirty instead of eight Frank said to me, "What shall I say?"

I said, "Say yes. Say yes." We were told not to tell anyone until the FBI had made an exhaustive investigation into his background. In the meantime, we had to plan how to get rid of our car, Jeep, boat, and find a home for the dog. We had to rent our house, have a garage sale, and close up Frank's office. Both of us had to resign from our boards.

We were often asked how a Wyoming cowboy become the Lieutenant Governor of American Samoa. In 1970 the Interior Department decided to set up a government in the territory of American Samoa based on our state system. Frank's twenty-two years in the Wyoming House of Representatives and the Senate qualified him to guide the Samoans in their new system. It was also equally important that both of us were from the West Coast of the U.S. The Samoans' past experience taught them that people from the more urbanized East Coast could not adjust as well to primitive conditions and the isolation. They would soon break their contracts and leave the island scrambling to replace them.

The Samoan experiences left us little time for boredom. Daily Pan Am flights brought many dignitaries at midnight from other South Seas islands, New Zealand and Australia. Among our visitors were many U.S. senators and representatives, and educators intrigued by the grade schools taught by television, family and friends. They were taken on tours and we entertained them. Our routine included learning about Samoan customs, and mores. We learned to design tapa boards and to make pottery. Our recreation included fishing and snorkeling over the beautiful coral reefs and shelling.

In 1975, after five wonderful years in American Samoa, Frank and I retired to Longboat Key, Florida. Many of our new friends from the East Coast of the United States were fascinated with the stories of our early life on a remote Wyoming ranch. It became the impetus to write *Eighty Miles From A Doctor.*